HISTORY

OF THE

TOWN OF FITCHBURG

MASSACHUSETTS

TO THE YEAR 1836

COMPRISING ALSO A

HISTORY OF LUNENBURG

FROM

ITS FIRST SETTLEMENT TO THE YEAR 1764

Rufus C. Torrey

HERITAGE BOOKS
2014

HERITAGE BOOKS

AN IMPRINT OF HERITAGE BOOKS, INC.

Books, CDs, and more—Worldwide

For our listing of thousands of titles see our website
at
www.HeritageBooks.com

A Facsimile Reprint
Published 2014 by
HERITAGE BOOKS, INC.
Publishing Division
5810 Ruatan Street
Berwyn Heights, Md. 20740

Originally published
Fitchburg:
Published by the Fitchburg Centennial Committee
E. & J. Garfield, Printer
1865

International Standard Book Numbers
Paperbound: 978-0-7884-0939-4
Clothbound: 978-0-7884-6061-6

PREFACE.

THE writer has been induced to undertake the present work by a desire to save from the oblivion to which they were hastening, some of the events connected with the history of this town. Many of these are treasured up in the memories of a few aged people, and must, in the course of nature, soon be inevitably lost, if not preserved in a connected and tangible form. Though the number of these relics of other days is now small, much information has been derived from them, and much more might have been obtained, had inquiries been commenced a few years earlier.

The writer has had full access to the proprietors' books, and to the town records of Lunenburg and Fitchburg. Oral and written information has been furnished with the utmost cheerfulness, by all those in possession of facts worthy of note. The labors of another who has preceded me in this department, have made my path one of comparative ease.

In 1831, Nathaniel Wood, Esq., in a series of lectures read before the lyceum of this town, gave an interesting and discriminating sketch of the events connected with its history. Many circumstances were collected and preserved by him, which would have been lost to the present writer. Unrestricted use of Mr. Wood's papers has been gen-

erously granted to me, who otherwise would not have been encouraged
to undertake the work. While then its merits, if it possess any, are
mainly to be ascribed to another; its faults and defects are chargeable
to me.

To N. F. Cunningham, Esq., and J. A. Marshall, M. D., the respective town clerks of Lunenburg and Fitchburg, this public expression
of my thanks is due for the readiness with which they have afforded
me every facility in their power, in the compilation of this work. To
other persons to whom I am more or less indebted for information, I
tender my grateful acknowledgements.

If I have succeeded in impressing any with the importance of pre-
serving the records and traditions of the early history of these towns,
and if those who peruse this work, derive from it a pleasure equal to
half of the labor I have spent in writing it, I shall not be without a
reward.

HISTORY OF FITCHBURG.

THE Town of FITCHBURG is situated in the north-eastern part of the County of Worcester, about forty-seven miles in a north-westerly direction from Boston, and twenty-four miles nearly north from Worcester. It is thirty miles west from Lowell, and four hundred and nineteen north-east from the city of Washington.

The general boundaries of the town are as follows:—north by Ashby, in the County of Middlesex, east by Lunenburg, south-east by Leominster, south by Leominster and an unincorporated district called No-town, and west by Westminster and Ashburnham. The average length of the town, from north to south, is a little more than six and a half miles, and the average breadth somewhat less than four and a half miles. It contains seventeen thousand eight hundred and seventy-nine acres, according to a survey made by Levi Downe, in 1830.

The general surface of the township is extremely uneven. It consists almost entirely of hills, some of which are very abrupt, and are of considerable magnitude. Rollstone, a hill lying immediately south-west of the village, rises abruptly three hundred feet above the bed of the stream which flows at its base; and there are other summits which rise still higher. Of meadow lands, there are scarcely any to be found in the limits of the town.

The soil is very broken, and much labor is required to subdue it thoroughly. When once put into a good state of cultivation, it has produced heavy crops of potatoes, and the various kinds of grain common to this section of the country. Wheat has been, and is still cultivated with considerable success. The town abounds in good pasturage lands, which, in consequence of the moist soil, seldom fail. Nearly the whole of the township was originally covered with a heavy growth of pine, which, being cut off, has given place to oak of different kinds, beech, chestnut, rock-maple, birch, ash, &c. Walnut was formerly abundant, but now it is not very common.

A strange neglect has prevailed in regard to the cultivation of trees for shade and ornament, and the beautiful and easily cultivated fruit trees of New England. Apples are common, and a few cherries may be seen; but peaches, rareripes, pears, grapes, plums, apricots, nectarines, strawberries, &c., which might be produced in abundance, and with but little care and expense, are almost wholly strangers among us. Not a little beauty would be added to the village, were its streets ornamented with the majestic elm; and not a little would be added to the comfort of the citizens, were their grounds plentifully stocked with the wholesome and delicious fruits of summer and autumn.

Rev. Peter Whitney, in his valuable history of Worcester County, remarks thus of Fitchburg:—"This is a very hilly and uneven, but fertile town. The hills are large, high and steep; however, on them there is not broken, poor and waste land. In general, the soil is excellent."

The soil of this town is a decomposition of mica slate and gneiss. The former produces a soil of a medium quality, and is generally well fitted for grazing. The soil of a greater part of Worcester County is based on gneiss, which differs from granite only in having a slaty structure. The soil resulting from the decomposition of this rock furnishes some of the most fertile and productive farms of the State.

The hills of the town (with the exception of Rollstone) are mostly formed of mica slate. Rollstone, which rises three hundred feet high, and is nearly a mile in circumference, is a mass of granite, and " might furnish enough to supply the whole state for centuries."* This granite has not been extensively quarried, on account of the little demand for stone. It has hitherto been principally used for door-steps, in building the " Stone Mill," and in constructing three excellent bridges over the Nashua. The six columns which support the front and projecting part of the " Nashua River Hotel," are of this granite. The hill is favorably situated for quarrying, and the stone is easily split into blocks of almost any size. This granite is of the same kind and color with that of Westford. Some of it is too coarse for architectural purposes ; but blocks can be obtained no wise inferior to the best of Chelmsford granite.

This granite is sold at the quarry, well dressed, at thirty-five and forty cents the superficial foot.†

The peculiar appearance of the rock composing Pearl Hill, in the north-eastern part of the town, formerly induced the belief that gold or silver ore might be found beneath the surface, and attempts were made to expose the supposed mines. But all search was fruitless. For the want either of funds or perseverance on the part of those engaged in this mining undertaking, the attempt was soon abandoned, and it has never since been resumed. Whitney, in his history of Worcester County, has the following pertinent remarks on this subject :—" In the present state of our population, riches, in these northern parts, are with much greater facility, procured from the surface of the earth, by the various instruments of cultivation, than from deep and latent mines of the richest ore. When the country becomes overstocked with inhabitants, and support from the soil shall not be so easily

---

*Hitchcock's Geology of Massachusetts, page 16.

† " The cost of hammering and fine dressing granite in Boston, in the style of the Tremont House, I have been credibly informed, is about thirty cents the superficial foot. Ordinary work is, however, from twenty-five to thirty cents. The cost of the blocks of the Quincy granite for the Bunker Hill monument, delivered at Char'estown in a rough state, was thirteen cents, three mills per foot, and the cost of the unhewn stone for the church built last year in Bowdoin street, Boston, was fifteen cents ; but six years before, the rough Quincy granite, for the United States' Branch Bank, cost two dollars per foot."—[Hitchcock's Geol. of Mass.

obtained, it is not improbable that from this mountain will be dug large
quantities of those shining metals, as every thing at present favors the
conjecture." The population of the place has not yet become so
dense as to make it necessary to have recourse to the precious metals,
that may be contained within the bowels of *Pearl Hill*, for their support; and it may be doubted whether the present day and generation
will witness that period. The promising indications of the existence
of such metals have not induced another search, though the desire for
their possession, which so strongly incited our fathers, has not
diminished in the breasts of their sons. The latter wisely regard the
solid granite of Rollstone as a more valuable possession.

Upon the elevation formerly known as Appletree Hill, situated
east and northeast of the village, there are indications of the existence
of mineral coal; and the high and increasing price of fuel will soon,
it is presumed, cause a thorough examination into the matter.

Till within a few years, the roads of this town were in a wretched
condition. The first settlers, as is usual in such cases, located their
habitations on the heights of the various hills; and for the convenience
of the inhabitants, the roads were laid out in a sinuous course from
one hill to another. The principal roads thus passed over the loftiest
hills in the town; and it would seem that generally the most direct
route between two places was avoided for the purpose of making the
public ways both crooked and uneven. Our fathers had as much ab-
horrence for a straight road, as nature *once* had for a vacuum. The
" flat rock road," which leads over the hill immediately north of the
village, and the road which passes over " Carter's hill," by the house
of P. Williams, Esq., were once the great thoroughfares between
Vermont and Boston. The former is now impassable to carriages of
modern construction, and the latter is but little used.

Within a few years, a great reform in this respect has taken place;
and the town is now as distinguished for its excellent roads, as formerly
it was for its bad ones. The reform was commenced by straightening
and otherwise improving the road leading to Leominster.* A new

---

*Measures have recently been taken for making still farther improvements on this route.

road to Ashburnham was opened in 1830. It generally follows the course of the river, and is a level and well made road. About the same time a new road was opened to Lunenburg, and communication with that place is now easy and agreeable. A new and comparatively level road has recently been opened between this place and Westminster. The roads which afford communication between the people of Fitchburg and their northern neighbors at Ashby, are hilly and crooked. A few years only will be suffered to elapse before the evil will be remedied. A great amount of travel passes through this town on the Boston and Keene route. Two excellent stone bridges on this road were built over the Nashua river, a few rods west of the village, in 1829. They are both built with three arches, having a span of twenty-five feet, and, with the embankments, cost over twenty-one hundred dollars. They were somewhat injured by the freshet of February 1835. In consequence of the foundations of the piers not being laid sufficiently firm and deep, they were undermined by the force of the water, and *settled* several inches. The travel over them, however, has not been interrupted, and no farther damage is apprehended from their slightly *twisted* condition. The beautiful stone bridge over the Nashua at the "Burbank Paper-Mill" was built in the Fall of 1834, at an expense of more than eleven hundred dollars. It has two arches, each with a span of thirty feet.

The town has daily communication, by means of *mail* stages, with Boston, Keene, and Lowell. Stages also depart three times a week for Springfield and Worcester, and return on alternate days. Accommodation stages also pass daily between this place and Boston.

There are no natural ponds in the limits of the town, though the neighboring towns of Westminster, Ashburnham, and Lunenburg are highly favored in this respect. The artificial ponds, formed by the dams on the Nashua at the various mill seats are all small, on account of the fall in this stream in the greater part of its course through the town. The only stream of much importance in the town, is the north branch of the Nashua,* the sources of which are in the towns of Westminster and Ashburnham. Westminster pond, lying about seventy rods southerly from the Congregational meeting-house in Westminster, contains more than one hundred and sixty acres; and Wachusett pond, lying at the base of the mountain of the same name, about three miles south-easterly from the centre of the same town, is nearly as large. Two small streams issue from these ponds, and soon uniting, pass the "narrows" and enter Fitchburg, flowing in a north-easterly direction. A stream from Ashburnham and Gardner flows through the westerly part of Westminster, and, being augmented by two other streams, known as Tophet Swamp brook and Beech Hill brook, takes an easterly direction, enters this town, and soon unites with the above mentioned streams from the ponds in Westminster.

Phillip's brook which has its source in Watatich and East ponds, in the easterly part of Ashburnham, flows in a southerly and south-easterly direction through the northern part of Westminster, and receiving several minor streams, passes into Fitchburg, and unites with the main stream about a mile and a half west of the village. These several streams, united, form the north branch of the Nashua. This continues in a north-easterly direction till it reaches the centre of the town, when it takes a south-easterly course and passes into Leominster. It receives several contributary streams in addition to those already mentioned. A small stream rises in the southerly part of the town, and runs into the Nashua a little below Sheldon's dam. L. Pratt's chair shop and saw-mill are located on this stream. Another small brook runs into the Nashua near to Sheldon's & Pillsbury's gristmill. A saw-mill is located upon it. Punch brook, of about the same size with the last named stream flows through the village and empties into the Stone mill pond. Four dams are built on it, two of these afford water power for a cabinet maker's shop, and a carriage maker's shop. The other two are at present unoccupied. Baker's brook

*This river and the plantation at Lancaster, were formerly called *Nashaway.* Nashua is a modern refinement, but by no means an improvement. The ancient name is much the better of the two, and it should have been preserved; but as Nashua has been universally adopted I have thought it proper to conform to the spirit of the times.

enters this town from Ashby. It flows in a south-easterly direction, nearly the whole length of the town, and receiving Pearl Hill brook, passes into Lunenburg and Leominster, and unites with the Nashua. Two saw-mills are located on it. Wanoosnock brook, which rises in Notown, runs through the southerly part of the town, and unites with the Nashua near the centre of Leominster. There is one saw-mill on it within the limits of Fitchburg. There are several saw-mills and other shops on the tributaries to the Nashua, which have been already mentioned.

Osborn's mills, on the Turnpike, are on the principal stream which comes from Westminster. A large number of shingles are made here. A saw-mill and grist-mill are at the same place. The latter is, however, but little used.

Perkins & Baldwin's Factory is on Phillips' brook, about one hundred and sixty rods above its junction with the Nashua, and not far from two miles west of the village. Shirtings of a good quality are manufactured here. The brook here, which is a constant stream, makes a fall of eighty feet in thirty rods. Sixteen looms are in operation at this place.

At the junction of Philips' brook with the Nashua is situated J. T. Farwell & Co's Scythe Manufactory. Dams are thrown across both streams, the waters of which are thus secured.

A. Crocker & Co's Paper-mill is located on the Nashua, at the distance of one and a half miles west of the village. A good head of water is secured here. At this establishment paper of various kinds, principally however printing and writing paper, is manufactured to a considerable extent. The same "privilege" furnishes water power to A. Kimball & Co's Scythe manufactory, situated a few rods below the paper-mill. The scythes manufactured by Messrs. Kimball & Farwell have had an extensive sale, and they are well known to be of a superior quality. Great numbers of them are sold annually.

Sheldon & Pillsbury's dam is located about one hundred and eighty rods below the one last mentioned. From this pond a trench has been dug, nearly one hundred and fifty rods in length, by means of which the water is conveyed to a saw-mill and grist-mill. A fall of twenty-two feet is obtained, and it may be considered perhaps as the best mill seat on the stream. The grist-mill is furnished with two runs of stones, a corn-cracker and a flour-bolter. A large quantity of grain is brought to this mill, some from a great distance. It is more particularly noted for the superior manner in which flour is bolted.

In this respect it is not inferior to any mills in this region. The average quantity of flour prepared here, during the past year, has been about five barrels per day. In the course of the present year it will probably be doubled.

Town & Willis' Cotton Mill is situated a few rods west of the common. Twenty looms are here in operation, in manufacturing 4-4ths sheetings. It is at present leased to Levi Sherwin.

The Fitchburg Woolen Mill owned by the same company as the cotton-mill last mentioned, occupies an eligible situation in the very centre of the village. It is a commodious building of brick, and furnished with all the necessary out-buildings. Sixteen looms are in operation; eight of which are for broadcloths, and eight for cassimeres.

Newton's Cotton Factory, about one hundred rods below the one last named, was formerly a manufactory for sheetings. Negro cloths are now the principal article manufactured.

The Stone Mill, a large granite building, is situated in that part of the village known as the Old City. It is four stories high, and occupied by Percy Atherton, as a Cotton Factory. It has forty looms for weaving sheetings.

Crocker & Gardner's Paper-mill generally known as the Burbank Paper-mill, is eighty rods farther down stream. A good head of water is obtained here. This mill is altogether used for the manufacture of wrapping paper. Two engines are kept in almost constant motion, night and day, to furnish pulp sufficient to supply one machine. Both of the Paper-mills in this town have, in connexion with their machines, a late improved drying cylinder. The paper passes from the machine over a heated cylinder (generally from four to six feet in diameter,) which completely dries it. At the same time it is cut into pieces, of convenient size, ready to be folded into reams. Water is also furnished at this dam for a workshop not connected with the Paper-mill.

Next on the stream, situated about two hundred and forty rods below the Paper-mill, is Poor's (formerly Slater's) Woolen Factory. Sixteen looms are in operation here; on six of which cassimeres, and on ten, broadcloths are woven.

A dam is again thrown over the Nashua about one hundred rods farther down stream. From this pond the water is conducted by a trench, about fifty rods in length, to the Woolen Factory occupied by Amos Hill. This is a brick building, erected within a few years. A part of the factory is occupied by A. Hill, who has twelve looms in operation in making broadcloths. In the part occupied by Alfred Messenger there are eleven looms employed in making negro cloths.

Commencing with Osborn's mills on the Turnpike, and including Perkins & Baldwin's Factory, which is not on the principal stream, there are twelve mill seats already occupied. Of these, four are sites for Cotton Factories, three for Woolen Factories, two for Paper-mills, two for saw and grist mills, and one for a Scythe Factory. This account does not include A. Kimball's Scythe Factory, which is supplied with water from A. Crocker & Co's pond. There are several saw-mills, turning lathes, work shops, &c., connected with most of the Factories above numerated. A dam has been built over the stream between A. Crocker's and Sheldon's dams, and a chair shop is about to be erected on the spot. It is calculated that there are five " privileges" yet unoccupied, between Osborn's mills and J. T. Farwell's Scythe Factory. There are also several other convenient places on the Nashua, where dams may be constructed. At the present time not one half of the water power which may be developed on this stream and its tributaries, is " improved."

Other manufactories and trades must be noticed briefly. Another chair shop has been opened in the village. Here also are carriage and coach makers, wheelwrights, carpenters, shoemakers, blacksmiths, window sash and blind makers, saddle and harness makers, trunk makers, two clock and watch makers and jewellers, book-binders and booksellers, apothecaries, stone cutters, hatters, bellows makers, brick makers, coopers, painters, (house, sign, carriage and ornamental,) masons, tailors, glaziers, a bakery, a tannery, a printing office, &c., &c. The first printing office was opened in 1830; since which time a newspaper has been published here. For a short period in 1834 three papers (two political and one religious) were printed. The present paper (Worcester County Courier) and printing office are owned by J. Garfield.

There are eight public stores, containing the usual variety of English, American, and West India goods, and two bookstores.

The Fitchburg Bank was incorporated in the year 1832, with a capital of $100,000, and went into operation in July of the same year. It has usually declared semi-annual dividends of $3\frac{1}{2}$ per cent. and the stock is about ten per cent. advance. Francis Perkins has been President, and Ebenezer Torrey, Cashier, of this institution from the commencement.

The number of inhabitants previous to the census of 1791, is a matter of uncertainty. When the town was incorporated, February 3d, 1764, it contained about forty families; and the population at this period may be estimated at two hundred and fifty. According to the census of 1791, it amounted to eleven hundred and fifty-one. The taxable *polls* in 1793 amounted to two hundred and sixty-eight,—at the same time eighteen towns of the County contained a greater number, and thirty towns a less. The population in 1800 was one thousand three hundred and ninety; in 1810, one thousand five hundred and sixty-six; in 1820, one thousand seven hundred and thirty-six; in 1830, two thousand one hundred and seventy-nine. Within the last ten years the population has increased in a greater ratio than at any former period; and at the present time the number of inhabitants may be estimated at twenty-six or twenty-seven hundred. The increase from 1791 to 1800 was two hundred and thirty-nine; from 1800 to 1810, one hundred and seventy-six; from 1810 to 1820, one hundred and seventy; from 1820 to 1830, four hundred and forty-three.

The principal circumstances which tended to retard the population of the town in the earlier period of its history, was the expense of maintaining and keeping in repair the roads and bridges. The broken and uneven nature of the soil rendered the construction of roads laborious and costly. The item for building and keeping in repair the several bridges over the Nashua and its tributaries, was not small. The art of constructing durable bridges was not understood in those days. They were built of frail and unsuitable materials, and were constantly in need of repairs. When built in the most approved style of those days, they were liable to be swept away by the first freshet. The rivers, which have since been the source of the wealth and prosperity of the town, were, in the opinion of its earlier settlers, its greatest evils. In 1793, according to Whitney's History, there had been built on the Nashua a saw-mill, a corn mill, a fulling mill, a clothier's works, a trip-hammer, and works for grinding scythes. These occasioned a great resort of people to the place, and from a considerable distance. At this period there was much travel through the place, by people on their way between Vermont and Boston. With these exceptions, there was nothing to give to the growth of the place an impulse beyond that of the neighboring towns. The people subsisted principally by husbandry; and the soil upon which they toiled, was by no means peculiarly excellent. The unsettled condition of the country, during the period of the commercial restrictions, and the last war with Great Britain, tended still further to check the business of the place. Manufacturing establishments. might have done a profitable business, but this was the period of their infancy in our country; and the experiment of introducing them was attended with that varied and uncertain success which usually marks the first efforts for finding new and untried channels for business and profit.

Many of those who found manufacturing a lucrative employment during the war, had their profits cut off and their business ruined at the termination of the contest, by the introduction of foreign goods, with which the markets were glutted, and with which they could not compete.

NOTE ON THE MANUFACTURES.—As the manufacture of cotton and woolen goods forms so important a branch of the business of the town, it has been thought that a more particular account of the time at which the several factories were erected and put into operation, would prove interesting.

The exact period when Dea. Amos Kimball and his cousin Ephraim removed from Bradford and settled within the limits of the present town of Fitchburg, is not known; but it was probably during the year 1745 or 6, when this town constituted a part of Lunenburg. Amos Kimball settled on the farm which Samuel Hale now occupies, and Ephraim lived on what is now known as the Storey farm. *They built the first dam across the Nashua* in this town, near the place now occupied by the "Stone Mill," and erected here a saw mill and a grist-mill. This primitive dam, the model of which might have been taken from the structures of the beavers, was a frail piece of workmanship, and was generally swept away by the annual freshet. After the close of the Revolutionary struggle, a fulling mill and clothier's works, a carding machine, and works for grinding scythes, were erected here. The building occupied by the carding machine was afterwards used for manufacturing satinets, and for other purposes—but to little extent, and less profit. These buildings have since given place to the excellent stone structure, which will be mentioned in the proper place.

A new dam of granite was built a few feet below the old one, in 1826.

The brick factory, now owned by Messrs. Town, Willis, and others, was the first factory erected in the town, and among the earliest (probably the second or third) built in this state. It was commenced soon after Slater's factory at Pawtucket, in the year 1807. A factory was built at New Ipswich, N. H. a short time previous; Plant's factory at Lancaster, and one at Peterborough, N. H. were undertaken very soon after. The dam belonging to the brick factory was built by Ephraim Kimball in 1807, and the factory was commenced at the same time by a company of about thirty individuals, who took shares in this novel experiment of spinning cotton.

The building which they erected, was thirty feet by sixty. The lower part was used as a workshop, while the upper was occupied by a picker, and was used as a store house for cotton. The Corporation (the company was incorporated in the winter of 1806–7,) employed one Robbins, who had had some experience at Slater's works in Pawtucket, to make patterns for castings, construct machinery, and " start" the mill. This Robbins usually drank a *quart of brandy* daily, and was not altogether a very amiable character. Being puffed up as master-workman and as the possessor of important secrets, he assumed an independent and overbearing demeanor, which was not very pleasing in the eyes of the Corporation. All the workmen here employed had to take shares in the concern, and when it became necessary to lay an assessment upon these, Robbins claimed an exemption, on the ground of being the most important man. To this the Corporation would not assent ; and thereupon the master-workman determined that they should feel his power. Instead, then, of hastening the completion of that part of the machinery which would be first wanted, he deliberately went to work upon that which would be needed last, and thus retarded the " starting" of the factory some time.

But Robbins soon found that he had over-estimated his own importance ; for some of the *enterprising* young workmen, by climbing the lightning-rod and descending the scuttle of the factory, got possession of his chest, which contained his important patterns, and made themselves acquainted with all the secret knowledge which the said chest contained. Hereupon Robbins was unceremoniously dismissed.

Afterwards an individual by the name of Field, who had been engaged at New Ipswich, N. H., was hired to take the immediate superintendance of the factory, which went into operation under his direction. The operations of the company did not appear to have been very profitable at first, in consequence of the imperfections of the machinery, and the great expenditures necessary in such experimental undertakings. In a company, too, of such heterogeneous materials, great unanimity could not be expected ; and complaints were frequently heard, and shares often passed from one owner to another.

In a few years, however, the Corporation began to do a more profitable business, machinery of an improved construction having been introduced, and the restrictions upon the commerce of the country, and the subsequent war operating in their favor.

The Corporation had committed a great oversight in not securing a proper title to their dam. The individual who built it was owner of the land on one side of the river, and the Corporation owned on the other side. The dividing line between them was in the middle of the river. This individual having lost money by building the dam, demanded four hundred dollars of the Corporation to cover his loss. This was refused. He then informed the Corporation that he was owner of one half of the dam, which he offered to sell them for the sum of twelve hundred dollars. The Corporation having neglected to comply with his terms, he sold his title to the dam and a piece of land (now occupied by Capt. Z. Sheldon's carpenter's shop,) for fifteen hundred dollars to two persons, who soon commenced building some works there. They made free use of the water, and finally cut away a part of the dam. This was a death blow to the Corporation. Their business was suddenly stopped when they were reaping an immense profit from it, and they were soon involved in a ruinous law-suit. An unusually large quantity of cotton on hand was, after some time, disposed of at a great sacrifice. They were suffering a loss of undoubtedly more than fifty dollars daily—perhaps nearer a hundred.

The question at issue between the Corporation and the owners of the other side of the river, was finally decided by referees against the former. The expenses of this suit and the heavy damages awarded against them were more than the Corporation were able to bear. It failed in 1816. In addition to the factory, they owned the two brick boarding houses, and the brick store now occupied by Messrs. Mc-Intire & Caldwell.

After the failure of the Corporation, their property was purchased by Messrs. Putnam & Perkins, for about one-third of its original cost. It remained in their hands, and the factory was kept in operation, till 1822, when it was purchased by Messrs. Town & Willis, who put in machinery for the manufacture of woolen goods. It has remained in their hands since that period. In 1834 it was enlarged by an addition of forty feet in length and thirty-eight in breadth.

The second attempt at cotton spinning, in this town, was made by Capt. Martin Newton. He had been employed by the Corporation, when their works were first put in operation. The location of the carding machine, near the site of the present stone mill, has already been mentioned. In this building Capt. Newton put in operation two spinning frames, on " Election Day," in the year 1810. The expense of fitting up this limited concern was about $1800,—and the profits at the end of the first year were but little short of $1000. It yielded an income of at least 60 per cent. on the capital invested. Cotton yarn, at this period, readily commanded eighty-five cents per pound.

This business proving to be so lucrative, Capt. Newton, in connection with Solomon Strong (at present one of the Justices of the Court of Common Pleas) and Jonathan Flint, (both of these latter then belonged to Westminster) erected, in the year 1812, the building now known as Newton's factory, and continued there the manufacture of cotton goods.

The dam at the " Rollstone (cotton) Mill " was built by Jonas Marshall and Dea. Ephraim Kimball* in the year 1794. *This was the second dam built across the Nashua.* At the same time they built a saw-mill ; and shortly afterwards clothier's works and a trip-hammer were built on the site of the blacksmith's shop a few rods below the factory. No vestiges of these now remain.

The Red (or Rollstone) Mill was built in 1813, by John and Joseph Farwell and Nehemiah Giles. When Messrs. Putnam & Perkins purchased the property of the exploded "Corporation," they bought the Rollstone Mill also, as the pond of the former intruded somewhat upon the water-wheel of the latter. It was owned by Gen. Ivers Jewett, and in 1833, it was purchased by Messrs. Town, Willis, and others.

*He was a son of that Ephraim who was among the earlier sett'ers of the town. Dea. Ephraim Kimball left a large fami'y, several of whom are now living in this town.

The factory on Phillips' brook, generally known as "Baldwin's factory," was built in the fall of 1814. The persons engaged in this undertaking experienced a fate common to many, who, about this time, embarked their whole fortune in cotton manufactories. Soon after the commencement of their operations, peace was declared between this country and England, and the company failed. The fall of the water at this place is very great. The *hole* occupied by the factory was extremely rugged and rocky, and great expense was incurred in clearing it out. The factory is supplied by two small ponds—the surface of the water in the upper one being nearly on a level with the steeple of the factory, which is about thirty rods distant.

The Red Woolen factory, situated about a mile southeasterly of the village, and now owned and occupied by Benjamin Poor of Boston, was built in 1823, by Tyler Daniels & Co. It was in their possession four or five years, when they disposed of their interest in it. After changing owners several times, it was purchased by Samuel Slater, whose heirs sold it to the present owner. For several years it was not in operation. It was put in operation again by John A. A. Laforest & Co., in 1834. An addition was made to this mill in 1827.

The Stone Mill (cotton) was built in 1826, by Oliver Fox, Esqr. It is very near, or partly occupies, the site of the first grist-mill and saw-mill erected in the town by Deacon Amos and Ephraim Kimball. The present lessee and owner of the machinery, is Percy Atherton.

The brick (woolen) factory at South Fitchburg was built by Hollis Hartshorn, in 1832. Soon after the commencement of the building, William Whitney of Boston became joint owner in the concern. It is now owned by him and Capt. Z. Sheldon. It is leased to Amos Hill, as has been mentioned in another place.

The Burbank paper-mill and dam (the third built across the Nashua) were built in the year 1804, by Thomas French. The mill went into operation the following year.

A. Crocker & Co's paper-mill was built in 1826; and the dam there was made in the previous autumn. This place was exceedingly rough and difficult of access. The dam alone cost $1500.

The above account embraces the most important items relating to the origin and progress of the manufactures of Fitchburg.

Previous to the commencement of the manufacture of woolen cloths in 1822, some attempts had been made in manufacturing satinets, in the Old City, but the scheme was a losing one, and was soon abandoned.

Saw-mills were built on several of the minor streams, in different parts of the town, at quite an early period.

When the town was in its infancy, the opinion was general, that it could never be a flourishing place, as its enterprise and prosperity would always be checked by the burthensome taxes necessary to keep in repair the roads and bridges. The Nashua river was considered as the curse of the place! The present condition and future prospects of the town are a singular commentary on the opinion of our fathers.

The number of ratable polls at this time is about 700. The militia is composed of three companies, viz—two standing companies and one of light infantry.

The town is divided into twelve school districts. From the School Returns furnished to the Legislature, for the year 1835, I gather the following statements:—The number of children attending Common Schools, from four to sixteen years of age is, males, 271; females, 289. Average attendance, 416. Children not attending Common Schools any portion of the year,—15 males, 26 females. Aggregate time of keeping school in all the districts is, in winter, 28 months, 21 days; summer, 28 months, 7 days. Number of male instructors, 11; female do. 14. Average wages per month, exclusive of board, winter, $16,67; summer, $4,30. Amount of money raised by tax for supporting Common Schools, $1,237,50. Estimated amount paid for tuition at the Academy and private schools, $705,00.

The Academy is a commodious, two-story building, situated a few rods easterly of the common. It was erected in 1830, at an expense of about $1200,00. It is furnished with two school rooms on the lower floor; the former of which will accommodate sixty-five scholars, and the latter thirty. The average number of scholars attending, for several years past, has been about thirty.

CIVIL HISTORY.

Before entering upon the civil history of the town, it may be proper to take a glance at the situation and condition of this part of the country, at the time when the white man first placed his foot upon it, and sought an abiding place and shelter in the then unknown wilderness.

What events transpired previous to this period, the imperfect traditions of the natives do not inform us. The elements of nature were at work upon the soil, but its mould was not disturbed by the arts of civilized life. Trees sprung forth, grew to a majestic height, and then fell to the earth in the natural progress of decay.

The Nashua wound its devious course through the forest, the stillness of which was not interrupted, save by the shout of the savage, the cry of the beast of prey, or the scream of the wild bird of the wilderness. The current of the stream may have been choked by the trunks of trees, hurled by the violence of the tempest into its bosom. The mass of accumulating water would then burst forth, perhaps seeking a new channel in its onward course. What changes have heretofore taken place in the course of the Nashua, we know not— running water is always wearing.

There is every appearance that the bed of the stream which flows by Messrs. Perkins & Baldwin's factory, once was situated ten or twenty feet higher than at present, in the ledge of rocks near their dam. But the changes, which have taken place on the surface of our township, are more fit speculations for the geologist. We cannot speak with certainty of its appearance, till after it was visited by the white man.

At this period we know that this section of the country was thinly peopled by several Indian tribes. A few years previous to the landing of our fathers at Plymouth, a deadly pestilence raged among the aborigines, and swept nine-tenths of them to their graves. The Indian population did not average one inhabitant to each square mile.

The Indians of New England were divided into five principal tribes, all of which extended their jurisdiction into the limits of the present county of Worcester. There were, also, several smaller tribes under their own sagamores or sachems; but they were all tributary to the larger tribes.

The Pequods, whose sovereign resided at New London, Ct., had dominion over the Nipmucks, in the southern and southwestern part of the county. The Narrhagansetts occupied what was then the colony of Rhode Island. They, also, had tribute from some of the Nipmucks. The Pokanokets, or Wampanoags lived in the Plymouth colony. Their sachem's seat was at Mount Hope (Haup) near Bristol. The celebrated Philip, or Metacom was their chief. They extended their authority over another portion of the Nipmucks. It is not probable that either of these tribes extended their jurisdiction so far north as Fitchburg.

The Massachusetts were the next great tribe northward, and extended from the bay of the same name to the Connecticut river. The Nashuas, in the vicinity of Lancaster, and the northern portion of the Nipmucks, were under this tribe. If this town was included in the territory of the Nashuas, it was under the jurisdiction of the Massachusetts; but this is not very probable, as the Nashuas consisted of only fifteen or sixteen families, residing on the interval lands of Lancaster, or near the ponds of Sterling.

The Pawtuckets dwelt in the northeastern parts of the state, on the banks of the Merrimack and its tributaries. This tribe probably extended over the northern part of the county. If this supposition be correct, then Fitchburg undoubtedly formed part of the territory of the Pawtuckets.

Again, it has been supposed that the town was in the territory of the Penicooks, who principally resided in the region about Concord, N. H. But there is not much foundation for the opinion that their realms extended so far south.

The Nipmucks, if ever an independent, were now a broken down tribe, as most of the neighboring sachems claimed sovereignty over them. They were a harmless, simple minded race, and many of them became converts to christianity, through the preaching of the celebrated Indian Apostle, Elliott. These Indians and the Nashuas conducted with good faith towards their white neighbors, till *King Philip's* war, in 1675, when they were induced to unite with him. When the Nashuas were broken up, most of them joined the Penicooks at the north.

The Indian population was so extremely sparse, when this territory began to be settled by the whites, that there is no reason to believe that the geographical lines of the different tribes were distinctly marked—they were determined rather by tacit consent or general understanding. Sometimes, when the hunting parties of one tribe pursued their game into the limits of another, or caught their fish in forbidden waters, then feelings of indignation were enkindled in the bosoms of the aggrieved party, and measures of retaliation were concerted. Hence feuds, not only between individuals, but between whole tribes, arose, and bloody wars were originated.

There do not appear to be any well authenticated accounts, which tend to show that the Indians of any tribe ever made any part of this town a permanent place of residence. Stone arrow-heads have been dug up in various places, and other implements of Indian manufacture have been found in the field opposite to the house of Capt. Philip F. Cowdin, but not in sufficient numbers to authorize a supposition that their owners ever permanently resided there. They have, however, left behind them sufficient relics for us to conclude that they were neither ignorant nor unmindful of the excellent shad, alewives, or salmon-trout, which sported in the waters of the Nashua, or of the deer and wild turkeys, which found a shelter and a covert under the branches of the majestic pines which towered above our hills.

It may be an amusing speculation to inquire when the soil of Fitchburg was first pressed by the foot of the white man. In 1643, but little more than twenty-two years after the landing of the Pilgrims at Plymouth, the region about Lancaster was in subjection to *Sholan,* sachem of the Nashuas. He had opened a species of traffic with the people of Watertown, and for greater convenience in this respect he invited Mr. Thomas King, and others residing there, to remove to the fertile regions of the Nashua. They complied with his advice, and commenced the plantation in 1643. In 1653, the town, then containing nine families, was incorporated by the name of Lancaster. From this time the inhabitants dwelt in peace, till the commencement of Philip's war, in 1675.

To the east of us, the town of Groton was incorporated in 1655. Beyond these points, which were on the verge of civilization, the white population did not extend for a considerable time. Perhaps some hunter from these frontier settlements, in his solitary pursuit after game, may have traversed our hills, and penetrated the unknown wilderness; but this is altogether conjecture.

February 10th, (O. S.) 1676, the Indians attacked Lancaster, and after destroying the settlement by burning the houses and murdering many people, they marched with the prisoners towards Canada. Among these was Mrs. Rowlandson, wife of the minister of the place. After her return from captivity, she published an account of her journeyings through the wilderness, under the title of "Twenty Removes." From this quaint work and other data, attempts have been made to trace her course. But the country being then entirely wild, and her accounts extremely vague in consequence—her mind at the same time being depressed by the hazards of her perilous situation, and by recollections of the recent calamity which had fallen so heavily upon her—nothing very satisfactory has been elicited. Her descriptions answer to three distinct routes, the most northern of which would carry her through Fitchburg.

From her account it appears that she spent the first night of her captivity on a small island in a river. This is supposed to be in Leominster. There is an island there answering very well to her description. The second night she passed upon a *high hill*—the third night in Narrhagansett, which is now Westminster—and on the eighth day of her captivity she arrived at a place now in New Braintree.

If then it be assumed that she staid the first night in Leominster, and the third night in Narrhagansett, there is every reason to believe that—independent of all tradition and all circumstances related by her—she passed the second night somewhere in the limits of the present town of Fitchburg. Taking all things into consideration, there is good foundation for the conjecture that she passed the second night on Rollstone hill. If this conjecture be true, what a scene must have been witnessed by her, on the summit of that hill, on the night of the 11th of February (O. S.) 1676. The merciless savages, exulting in their success, were celebrating the massacre which they had inflicted upon the innocent people of Lancaster, and testifying by their dreadful rites and hellish orgies, their joy at shedding human blood. In the midst of them sat the lone white woman—her spirit crushed to the earth by the weight of her sudden and overwhelming calamities. Torn from her husband, sorrowing for the destruction of her kindred and friends, with no comforts to supply her necessities— no shelter to protect her from the wintry blasts—and with a dread of a hopeless captivity in prospect, she was entirely dependent upon the "tender mercies" of the savages, the murderers of her children.

I will now leave these matters of uncertain speculation, and proceed with the dull relations of history.

Previous to the incorporation of this town, under the name of Fitchburg, in 1764, it formed a part of Lunenburg. To begin, then, at the beginning, and acquire a knowledge of our origin, it is necessary to search into the early records of Lunenburg, in the transactions and events of which town the people who inhabited what is now Fitchburg, had an equal interest, and an equal share.

In Whitney's "History of Worcester County," the account of Lunenburg commences as follows:—"On the 4th of November, 1719, the General Court, at the request of a number of gentlemen, made a grant to them of this territory for a valuable consideration," &c. Who these "gentlemen" were, is not known; but it is presumed they were among those whose names are preserved in the proprietors' books, as the earliest settlers. The "valuable consideration" above mentioned, will be made known by the terms of the grant. Furthermore, this order, or grant of the General Court, is of great importance; for it is not only the foundation of our municipal rights, but it is the basis upon which rest all the titles to real estate in this town and Lunenburg. I will therefore give it entire, from an exact copy of the original records, as furnished by the Secretary of the Commonwealth:

" Anno Regni Regis Georgii Magnæ Britanniæ, &c. Sexto.

At a great and General Court or Assembly for his Majesty's Province of the Massachusetts Bay in New England, begun and held at Boston, upon Wednesday, the twenty-seventh of May, 1719, and continued by Prorogation to Wednesday, the fourth of November, 1719, and then met; being their second session.

Monday, December 7, 1719.

In the house of Representatives, the vote for granting two new towns was brought down from the board, with Amendments, which were read and agreed to—And the said vote is as follows, viz :—

Voted that two new Towns, each containing a Quantity of land not exceeding six miles square, be laid out in as regular Forms, as the Land will allow; to be settled in a defensible manner, on the Westerly side of Groton West line, and that William Tailor, Samuel Thaxter, Francis Fulham, Esqrs., Capt. John Shipley, and Mr. Benjamin Whittamore, be a Committee fully impowered to allot and grant out the land contained in each of the said towns, (a lot not to exceed Two hundred fifty acres) to such persons, and only such as will effectually settle the same within the space of three years next ensuing the laying out and granting such lots by the Committee, who are instructed and directed to admit eighty families or persons in each Town at least, who shall pay to the said Committee for the use of the Province, the sum of Five Pounds for each allotment, which shall be granted and allotted as aforesaid; and that each person to whom such lot or lots shall be granted or laid out, shall be obliged to build a good Dwelling House thereon and inhabit it; and also to break up and fence in three acres of land the at least within the Term of three years; and that there be laid out and reserved for the first settled Minister, a good convenient Lot;* also a Lot for the School,† and a ministerial lot,‡ and a lot for Harvard College,§ of two hundred and fifty acres each; and that the Settlers be obliged to build a good, convenient House for the Wor-

---

 *This lot was where T. & J. Dunsmoor now live, near the north burial place.

 †The School lot was in the N. W. part of Lunenburg; and a portion of it came within the limits of Fitchburg.

 ‡The Ministerial lot was so divided that it is now difficult to fix the precise situation of the several parts.

 §The College lot was in the N. N. E. part of Lunenburg.

ship of God in each of the said Towns, within the term of four years ;
and to pay the charge of necessary surveys, and the Committee for
their service in and about the premises ; and that the Committee give
public notice of the time and place when and where they will meet to
grant allotments.

Consented to—   SAML. SHUTE."

These two townships were designated by the Committee appointed
to allot and grant them out, as the North and South townships. The
former was afterwards incorporated by the name of Townsend, in the
county of Middlesex. The south township included the present towns
of Lunenburg, Fitchburg and a large portion of Ashby.

Whitney, and every other authority which I have seen, assert that
this grant was made on the *fourth of November*, 1719. A copy of
the grant is given on the first page of the book, containing an account
of the doings of the Committee. It is as follows :—

"At a Great and General Court or Assembly for his Majestie's
Province of ye Massachusetts Bay, held Nov. 4, 1719, in ye House
of Representatives," &c. This error of thirty-three days as to the
date of the grant was probably made either by the Committee's being
furnished with an imperfect copy of the act, or by a mistake of Francis Fullam, the Committee's clerk, in copying it into their book.
This latter was probably Whitney's authority, and it is not unlikely that
others have followed him. However, the authority of the records of
the General Court is not to be doubted. The act .passed the House
of Representatives and received the signature of the Governor on the
7th of Dec. 1719, old style, which corresponds with the 18th of Dec.
new style.

Whitney's account thus proceeds :—"There is a hill, in the middle
of the town, called *Turkey Hill*, on account of the great number of
wild turkeys which frequented the place in that day. It still retains
the name ; and gave denomination to the whole tract previous to its
incorporation." This account of Lunenburg in Whitney's History,
(which was published in 1793) was entirely prepared by Rev. Zabdiel
Adams, then minister of Lunenburg, and certainly a good authority
in the matters of his own day. This hill is now called " Clark's Hill,"

and is situated about two hundred rods southeasterly from the meeting house. I have enquired of several people who lived in Lunenburg previous to the publication of Whitney's history, and hardly one is to be found who recollects that any one hill in particular was called *Turkey Hill*, but they say that Turkey Hills was the name given to "all the hills around"—not only to the hills in Lunenburg, but to the loftier hills in Fitchburg, which were equally the resort of immense numbers of wild turkeys, which found a favorite food in a plentiful supply of chestnuts and acorns there abounding. One or two individuals, however, are quite certain that Clark's Hill was once called Turkey Hill; and it is their impression that it went by both names—that it generally was called Clark's Hill, though aged people still clung to its ancient designation. The name of Turkey Hill is now entirely superseded.

There is indubitable evidence that the tract included in the whole south township was called, not Turkey Hill, but Turkey Hills. In the "Account of the General Courts Committees Proceedings," written in 1720, it is so called. And in every other place where it occurs, it is written "Turkey Hills."

What Indian name was given to this territory, is not known; but the first name applied to it by white men, was Turkey Hills.

When this order or grant of the General Court passed, Dec. 7th, 1719, there was but one family residing in the territory of Turkey Hills. The head of this family was Samuel Page—universally designated by the honorable title of "Old Governor Page." This pioneer of the wilderness and patriarch of Turkey Hills was born, as I have been informed, in this section of the country (probably in East Cambridge,) in 1671 or '2, and removed at an early age to South Carolina. From thence he returned in poverty, to Groton, in this state, where he remained but a short period, and, in the summer of 1718, moved westward into what was afterwards Lunenburg, where he remained till his death in 1747.*

---

*The inscription upon his grave stone, executed in rude capitals, reads as follows:
"Here lies buried ye body of Mr. Samuel Page. He was ye first that settled in this town, who departed this life Sept. ye 7, A. D. 1747, in ye 76 year of his age."

When the General Court's Committee, (as they were styled) first visited the place in Dec. 1719, in the performance of their duty, they found Governor Page, whose faithful subjects were composed of his wife Martha, and several promising children, occupying a comfortable habitation on the southerly side of Clark's hill, a few rods to the rear of the barn belonging to the farm of Micah Marshall. It is directly opposite to the principal grave yard, little more than one mile in a southeasterly direction from the meeting house. Old Governor Page exercised not a little taste in the selection of his place of abode; for it is not only one of the most beautiful situations, but the land thereabouts constitutes one of the best farms in the town. He had, however, no title to the land which he was cultivating, for it was then public domain, and belonged to his Majesty's Province of the Massachusetts Bay. Accordingly, when the Committee met at Concord, in 1720, for the purpose of granting out lots, Samuel Page purchased one for himself, and one for his son Joseph. This Joseph was employed as a "chainman," when the town was first surveyed, and probably was about twenty years old. I am inclined to think that he was the Governor's eldest son. This dignitary's nearest neighbors were at Groton on the east, at Lancaster on the south, and on the borders of the Connecticut river on the west. The record of the births of his children commences in 1719, and enumerates six. Previous to this period there were born Joseph, Daniel, Nathaniel, David, John, and probably one or two more. One or more of them settled in Shirley. Joseph resided all his days in Lunenburg. One of them, (David) as I have been told, removed to the northerly parts of Vermont, and was the first settler of the town of Lunenburg, in Essex county. It is reported that he afterwards returned to his native state, and dwelt in Petersham.

An elderly gentlemen of Lunenburg, from whom these data were derived, remarked that he thought that the descendants of the last mentioned son had not entirely disappeared at the present day, and, in support of his opinion, related the following :—This Page, having a roving disposition and a speculative cast of mind, took it into his head, when quite young, that he could make more money by trading with the Indians, than by cutting down forest trees and cultivating the soil. Accordingly, he directed his course towards Canada, and commenced purchasing beaver and otter skins of the ignorant natives upon this principle,—that his foot weighed just *four* pounds and his hand *one* pound. This they seemed to doubt, but were soon satisfied by his making the declaration that it was as fair for one party as the other, since he weighed off to them, by the same weights, his powder, tobacco, shot, &c. This grand field for making an honest living was, however, soon closed; for some other traders coming that way, explained the trick to the Indians, and the Old Governor's speculating son had to decamp very suddenly—weights and all—to save his life.

It appears from the town records of Lunenburg, that "John Page, ye son of Samuel Page, died at Jamaica, being there on the Spanish expedition, Dec. 29th, 1740, as they hear."

David Page was undoubtedly among the earliest—perhaps the first of the settlers in that part of Lunenburg which is now Fitchburg. The birth of his eldest child is dated Oct. 1735. Some of the aged people of this town think that the first settlement made within our present precinct, by a white man, was on the place now owned by James L. Haynes—and that the occupant was sometimes called Governor Page. Others say that David Page lived there, but from how early a period they cannot tell. Perhaps the title of Governor, appended to this Page, was a hereditary privilege, or these informants may have blended the accounts of the two Pages in their minds. There can be but little doubt as to the residence of Old Governor Page near the centre of Lunenburg; for the land on which the first pound was built, and for a "passage to and from the same," was purchased of him, and the Governor himself was elevated to the office of pound-keeper.

There is, however, strong *circumstantial* evidence that the first settlement within what is now Fitchburg, was made by a man named Page—that his house stood a few rods westerly of the house of James L. Haynes, a short distance south of the present travelled road,

and near the small brook which flows there. This house was "garri-
soned," that is, sticks of timber, hewn on two˙ sides to about the
thickness of six inches, were firmly driven into the ground so close
together as to touch. This kind of barricade extended around the
house at the distance of about ten feet from it. Port-holes were made
through this of sufficient dimensions to allow the fire of musketry.
These fortified houses, called *Garrisons*, were frequently a good
defence against the attacks of the natives. This Page turned the
above mentioned small brook from its natural course, and made it flow
for some distance under ground, and then through his garrison. This
was done that, if menaced by the savages, he might sit securely in
his habitation and defy their efforts.

Having thus treated of the family of Old Governor Page, the consideration of the affairs pertaining to the township of Turkey Hills
may be resumed.

The Committee appointed by the act of Dec. 7th, 1719, to allot
and grant out the township, commenced their duties on the 21st of the
same month, and began the survey. Besides other expense incurred
by the Committee, the future proprietors were charged with the sum
of 12*s.* 6*d. old tenor;** "for Bisket, Cheese & Jenger to carry into ye
woods." The survey was resumed and completed in April of the
following year.†

---

*As many of my readers, at the present day, would probably find it difficult to determine the dif-
ference between "Old Tenor" and "Lawful Money," I will here add that in the year 1702, recourse
was had in the New England provinces to a paper currency, to support the expenses of government,
and furnish a substitute for a circulating medium. The bills purported that they would be redeemed
at a certain time, which was done at first, but it soon became customary to redeem them by new
emissions. This being done pretty liberally, they began to depreciate in value. In Massachusetts,
where their value was kept up better than in the other provinces, the depreciation was at the rate of
seven and a half for *one* in specie. This currency acquired the name of *Old Tenor*—seven shillings
and six pence being equal to only one shilling in silver, which was called "Lawful money," or nine
pence sterling of Great Britain.

In the year 1750, the government of Great Britain made a grant of a sum of money to Massachusetts, to remunerate the province for its exertions in the late war with France. Governor Hutchinson
proposed that this sum, which was sent over in dollars and parts of dollars, should be appropriated
to redeem the whole of the bills of credit of the province. This proposition, after much opposition,
was carried into effect ; and eventually it was productive of much good. Accordingly the circulation
of Old Tenor bills was finally stopped on the 31st of March, 1750. The last large emission of Old
Tenor bills was made by Governor Shirley, in order to defray the expenses of the expedition against
the island of Cape Breton, in 1745. This he did contrary to the express orders of the king to put a
stop to them ; but as the plan was successful no notice was taken of this breach of orders.

†It will be recollected that the Committee were directed to make the new township six miles *square*.
An inspection of the map of Lunenburg shows that this order was not executed. A corner of Leominster projects considerably into the southwest part of the town. When the second grant was made

On the 11th of May the Committee met at Concord, when the grantees entered their names for lots. They were obliged to pay at this time the sum of fifty shillings, old tenor, ($1.11) and obligated themselves to pay a like sum when they should finally draw their lots. If any individual refused to pay the last fifty shillings, he incurred a forfeiture of his lot, and of his first payment. The eighty lots were subscribed for, and the sum of 183*l*. 10*s* ($81.54) paid. Of the eighty individuals whose names were subscribed, seventeen belonged to Concord, fifteen to Groton, four to Needham, and the others to Newbury, Bradford, Reading, Boxford, Weston, Watertown, &c. Only one person's residence is put down at "Turkey Hills." This is Samuel Page, who subscribed for two lots—one for himself, and one for his son Joseph.

In May, 1721, the Committee again met at Concord, when the grantees drew their lots and paid for them in full. At this time five more grantees had been admitted, notwithstanding that the south township was "almost full." The number of grantees was subsequently increased to ninety.

It will be recollected that, according to the act of the General Court, each grantee was to receive two hundred and fifty acres. Twenty-two thousand five hundred acres would thus be disposed of. Then a lot was reserved for the first settled minister, for the school, for Harvard College, and there was a ministerial lot. At the first division, forty-five acres, "and that to be the standard of the best land," were allotted to each man—and if any happened to be of an inferior quality, five or more acres were added to it, "to make each lot equal."

This, it will be perceived, was taking but a small portion of the whole township. Accordingly, in January, 1724, a second division of about sixty acres additional was made. The meadows, were also divided into lots and annexed to the several "upland" lots; and thus

to Lancaster in 1713, (which grant was incorporated into Leominster in 1740) the Indians and whites, who "ran" the line, first watered their horses at Massapog pond, and then proceeded in a straight line to the southern point of Oonkeshewalom pond. This was the boundary line between the domains of the whites and natives.

34 HISTORY OF FITCHBURG.

they proceeded, making division after division, till nearly all the township of Turkey Hills was taken up by the original proprietors, or their assigns.

There is one circumstance connected with the grant of the General Court worthy of notice. The limits of the new township, according to that act, were not to exceed six miles square. Yet Turkey Hills embraced the present towns of Lunenburg, Fitchburg, and not a small portion of Ashby. It would puzzle a surveyor of the present day not a little, to discover how the worthy and conscientious progenitors of Turkey Hills contrived to get all this territory in a space of six miles square; for Fitchburg alone is more than six and a half miles long, and nearly four and a half broad—Lunenburg is of about the same size—and add the part afterwards set off to Ashby in 1767, and we have a territory equal to twelve miles in length and six in breadth, containing, at the least calculation, forty-five thousand acres.

No one, however, seems to have found fault with the survey, and certainly people at this late period, ought to remain satisfied with it.

In 1724 the grantees began to move into the town and occupy their respective lots. The first house built by Old Governor Page has already been mentioned. The second dwelling house,* as I have been told, was built by Edward Hartwell, Esqr.,† on or near the place

*I have not satisfactorily ascertained whether this house, or the one near the centre of the town, (marked 115 on the map of L.) owned by B. G. Whiting, and occupied by the Widow Goodridge and Daniel H. Humphries, was erected first. The latter was undoubtedly built as early as 1724, by Thomas Prentice, Esq., and was afterwards, and for a long period, occupied by Capt. Joshua Hutchens, as a public house.

†He was not only one of the earliest settlers, but for a long period he was deservedly one of the most influential persons of the place. He possessed a strong mind and an education superior to that of most of his fellow citizens. He was continually called upon to fill the most important offices in the town. He was one of those individuals, whose sound judgment and energy so well qualify them to take the lead in the affairs of a new settlement, when the influence of such persons is so essential to its prosperity. Whenever any important or extraordinary business was to be accomplished, Edward Hartwell was called upon to take the charge of it. He passed through several grades of office in the militia, and finally attained the dignity of major—an office at that time of more importance than that of a major general at the present day. In this capacity he took the lead in scouring the woods, when the people were alarmed by the movements of the Indians. He was a justice of the peace; and, in 1750, he was appointed a Judge of the Court of Common Pleas, which office he held till 1762. He was the representative of the town for a great number of years, even till he was upwards of eighty years of age. He was also a deacon of the church, "and, finally he died," as Whitney's History says, "in the ninety-seventh year of his age, as full of piety as of days."

now occupied by Stephen Gibson. It is about three and a half miles in a southerly direction from the centre of Lunenburg, on the Lancaster road. This individual, who exercised a great influence over the rising fortunes of the new township, came from Lancaster as early as 1724—perhaps earlier. The third was built by Dea. Philip Goodridge, on the place now occupied by his grandson, Phinehas Goodridge, on the road leading to Lancaster, about three miles in a southerly direction from the middle of Lunenburg. This house was built in the Autumn of 1724, or early in 1725. This Dea. Goodridge died in January, 1729, and, as I have been informed, was the first person interred in the principal grave yard of Lunenburg.* I find the deaths of several individuals recorded previous to this time, but where they were buried I do not know.

At a meeting of the General Court's committee, March 16th, 1726, it appears from information then laid before them, that there were twenty-six houses raised, "and ten of them settled and inhabited." Of these, though the larger portion was probably near the centre of Lunenburg, some may have been in that part which is now Fitchburg. But this is a very doubtful matter.

Among the names which appear on the records at an early date, are those of Benoni Boynton,[†] John Grout,[‡] Moses Gould, Samuel Johnson,[§] Josiah Willard,[||] Nathan Heywood,[¶] Jonas

---

*The inscription upon his grave stone reads thus :—

" Here lyes ye Body of Mr. Philip Goodridge (2d son of Mr. Joseph and Martha Goodridge) Who was born at Newbury and died at Lunenburg, Jan. 16, 1728-9 in the 60 year of his age. The first Man interred in this Place."

[†]He probably lived near where O. & J. Peabody now reside, about one and a half miles in a direction N. N. W. from the meeting house.

[‡]He had no fixed habitation, and probably never owned any real estate in Lunenburg. He was a speculating, moveable being, and, if any thing, was a pettifogger by trade.

[§]This Johnson is said to have lived where Luther Farwell now lives—about half a mile northeasterly from the Methodist meeting house.

[||]Capt. (afterwards Col.) Josiah Willard lived on the "Billings place," on the Lancaster road, a little more than two miles in a southerly direction from Lunenburg meeting house. He was a worthy man and had a great share of influence in the affairs of the infant settlement.

[¶]Nathan Heywood "settled" in the southern xtremity of the town, on the Lancaster road, where Oliver Whitney now dwells. He was a man of considerable note, having been appointed Deputy Sheriff, and afterwards Crier of the courts. He also kept in his house what, in those days, was dignified with the name of store, but on a very limited scale.

Gillson, Daniel Austen,[*] Joshua Hutchens, Thomas Prentice,[†] &c., &c.

Several years after the grant of the General Court, much complaint began to arise concerning the speculations which now began to be manifest among the original proprietors—for then, as in modern days, there appeared a strong desire of turning every thing into a money-making matter. Several of the purchasers, totally disregarding the conditions of the grant, and the injunctions of the Committee, neglected to perform any labor on their lots, and kept them from others likely to settle them. Inasmuch as they "traded them from one man to another, for excessive gain and prices, which practice was directly contrary to the written conditions and provisos upon which each person had his lot of the Committee," these latter proceeded to declare several lots forfeited, and sold them to other persons, from whom more obedience might be expected. After this summary proceeding, no more complaint was made concerning land speculations.

In November 1727, the General Court's Committee voted that the proprietors should forthwith proceed to the erection of a meeting house, to be not less than forty-five feet in length and thirty-five in breadth. From the diminutive size of this house it may be inferred that Turkey Hills, at this period, did not contain many families; yet they had already conceived thoughts of rejecting the further tutelage of the Committee appointed by the Great and General Court, and of setting up for themselves. They began to bestir themselves in the matter of procuring an act of incorporation, and the meeting house, proposed by the Committee, was not built. Yet they were not entirely without religious instruction, though they had no meeting house. May 15th, 1728, Rev. Andrew Gardner was settled as minister of Turkey Hills. The meetings, of course, were held in private dwellings.

Mr. Gardner was graduated at Harvard University in the year 1712. In the Autumn of 1719 he was ordained the first minister of

---

[*]Daniel Austen's habitation was where Calvin Eaton lately lived.

[†]The house built by Thomas Prentice, Esqr., and afterwards occupied by Capt. Joshua Hutchens, has already been mentioned in a preceding note.

Worcester. Here he remained till his dismission in October, 1722. Where he was during the interval between this time and his instalment at Turkey Hills, I do not know. He built and occupied the house now standing on the west side of Clark's Hill, and now the residence of the heirs of David Wood, 2d. It has quite an air of antique decay about it—a small portion of the old diamond form glass still remaining in some of the windows.

It was voted to raise the sum of 80*l*. ($35.55) on landed estate, for the annual salary of the minister for the next six years. This is apparently a very inadequate sum; but it will be recollected that money then, in consequence of its scarcity, was much more valuable than now—transactions between individuals being carried on principally by barter,—and that it was intended that the minister should derive his principal support from the lands appropriated by the General Court. Dissatisfaction soon arose between Mr. Gardner and his people. He accordingly asked for a dismission, which the town voted in February, 1732; and the church received his acquittance and gave him a discharge from his pastoral relations in the November following.* He thus continued in the pastoral office about four and a half years, and gave his receipt for his settlement and salary during this period, to the town, for the sum of 394*l*. 12*s* ($175.32.) He remained in the town several years after this, and was employed as the first schoolmaster—the school being kept in his own house. He was also allowed the privilege of building, at his own charge, "a sufficient pew at the right hand of going in at the great doors of the meeting house"—

---

*The following is a copy of a request or proposition submitted by Mr. Gardner to his church, September, 1730.

To the Brethren of the Church of Christ in Lunenburg:

Beloved Brethren—I cannot but think, from what I have heard, and also from what I have observed, of the transactions and behaviour of this people relating to me and my affairs, that there is not that affection borne towards me that there should be from a people to their Gospel minister, or that there is where a people are likely duly to profit under their minister,—the consideration whereof has been very grievous and discouraging to me, and therefore think it best to separate;—and if effectual care be taken that my dues be honestly paid me, the first minister's lot with its appurtenances be put upon record and accepted, and a sufficient Pew at the right hand of going in at the great doors of the meeting house, I shall be free to be dismissed from my pastoral relation, office, and obligation to you, as soon as it can regularly be performed.

From your loving Pastor, who wisheth you the Divine direction and blessing, and desires your prayers for the same to him.   ANDREW GARDNER, *Pastor*.

Lunenburg, Sept. 18, 1730.

which was a very honorable station. He finally removed to New Hampshire, nigh to Connecticut river, where he died at a very advanced age.

The reasons of this dismission, so far as I have been able to learn them, appear to be these:—He was not a man of that grave and sober demeanor, which the people of his time thought essential to the sacredness of his office. He was apt to indulge in a levity of manner on the Sa'.bath, which was not in keeping with the solemnity of the day. He had also quite a predilection for hunting, and, it is said, wild turkeys and other game, even on the Sabbath, sometimes bore testimony of his skill as a marksman. For the truth of these reports I cannot vouch.

On the first day of August, 1728, the proprietors of Turkey Hills, with their lands, were incorporated by the name of Lunenburg, in the county of Middlesex. It was so named in compliment to George II who, in the preceding year, succeeded to the British throne. One of his titles was Duke of Lunenburg, he having a town or province of that name in his German dominions.

The first "town" meeting was held at the house of "Ensign Jonathan Willard,"* on the 19th of the same month, by authority of an order in Council, directed to " Capt. Josiah Willard, a principal inhabitant," &c. The first "Selectmen" were James Colburn, Josiah Willard, Hilkiah Boynton, Ephraim Pearce, Samuel (Gov.) Page.

In Sept. it was voted to raise the sum of £200 ($88.88) for building and finishing a meeting house, "so far as it is will do or answer therefor." This, the first meeting house, a building of small dimensions and a mere shell, was located a few rods to the north of the dwelling house of Edmund Cushing, and nearly opposite to the present Town Meeting House. A pulpit and "a body of seets" were built in 1731. The persons, "*preferred*" to have pews, had to build them at their own cost. A committee was chosen "to state places for building the pews, and order who shall have them," and it was further

*The house which first had the honor of containing the people of Lunenburg assembled in their corporate capacity, is now owned by Jacob Hadley, and situated on the Lancaster road, about one and a half miles distant from the meeting house.

ordered " that the rule the committee shall go by shall be according to the inhabitants' *improvements* and *stations*, and having some regard to *pay*." In April, 1733, in was voted to finish the galleries in the meeting house, and to build " stears up into them."*

The worthy people of Lunenburg took good and seasonable care that all vagrants and rogues should meet with their deserts; and accordingly in 1732, they voted " the sum of eight shillings for building a pair of *stocks*."

In 1729 they chose Capt. Josiah Willard their agent " to join with others to consider what may be best in order to divide the county of Middlesex." This object was effected April 2d, 1731, when Worcester County was incorporated. At this time grand and " Petty" jurymen were chosen by the people in town meeting assembled.

In a little more than two years after this, attempts were made to form a new county out of the counties of Worcester and Middlesex, of which Groton was to be the shire town. These attempts in a short time were abandoned.

The subject of schools appears to have first engaged the attention of the town in 1732, when Rev. Mr. Gardner was employed to teach a school for three months, in his own house. Next year it was kept at the houses of several individuals in rotation, and in Dec. 1734, 40*l.* ($17.77) were voted for a " Lawfull School," " for the year past and present." In 1735 the selectmen were directed to provide for a school " according to the best manner for the town's *safety* and interest," and the year following they were directed " to hire *School Dames* as they shall see fit, and otherwise as the Law requires." In 1737, 50*l.* and in 1738, 60*l.* ($26.66) were appropriated towards the support of schools. During six months of the latter year, " School Dames" were employed.

In 1740 the town resolved to build two " school housen," one at the north and one at the south end. But this vote was soon reconsidered,

---

*In 1736, the town " granted all the room behind the front gallery in the meeting house to Jona. Wood, Samuel Reed, Phinehas Osgood, Ezekiel Wyman, David Page, Stephen Boynton, John Fitch & Jona. Abbott, for to build a long pew or seet for themselves and wives forever to set in."

and they resolved to build one school house near the meeting house—
and all persons residing more than two miles distant from it, had
liberty to support schools among themselves, the money which they
paid to the town for this purpose being refunded to them. Whether
this school house was ever built I do not know, as, for the several
subsequent years, the school committee were directed to provide places
to keep the school in, and to move it as they thought best.

Some years after this, the town resolved to build four school houses
in the four quarters of the town, but they could not determine upon the
place for their location. The schools continued to be kept in different
quarters of the town till Fitchburg was set off. The money for their
support was gradually increased from 25l. to 50l. in bills of credit.
The exact sum cannot easily be estimated in consequence of the
depreciation in the value of the bills.

Immediately after the dismission of Mr. Gardner, in the Autumn
of 1732, Rev. David Stearns,* of Watertown, was hired to preach.
He was invited to become the Pastor of Lunenburg in the February
following, and he was ordained in April.† He received a settlement
of 300l., 200l. of which were paid the same year and 100l. the
following year. His salary was to be 120l. in "bills of credit," per
annum, to be increased 5l. per annum, till it should amount to 140l.
" to be qualified by the present value."

Generally speaking, during the ministry of Mr. Stearns, the town
enjoyed a profound peace in their ecclesiastical affairs. They went
through the process of building a new meeting house, and of course
were not exempt from the troubles and divisions usually consequent
on these occasions.

Mr. Stearns occupied the dwelling house which stands immediately
north of the present Methodist meeting house, where John Thompson

---

*Mr. Stearns was graduated at Harvard College in 1728. He was one of fourteen children (by the
same mother) who followed their father to the grave. Mr. Stearns himself became the father of thirteen children. One of his daughters subsequently was married to Rev. Zabdiel Adams, of Lunenburg,
and was the mother of eleven children.

†On this occasion the sum of 23l. 18s. 6d. " was paid to Col. Josiah Willard for entertaining the
Ordination Councell." It was raised, " one half on the Pools, and one half on the Estates"—as the
Records state.

now dwells. In 1736 and '7, and several subsequent years, additional sums of 25l. and 30l. were appropriated to "make good" his salary, in consequence of the depreciation of money.

The currency, at this period, was in a wretched condition. Bills of credit had been issued so early as 1690, to meet the expenses of the expedition against Canada. The expense of the wars for several years caused an extensive issue of these bills, beyond the means of the province to redeem them, and they consequently began to sink in value. There was not specie enough, even in the country, to redeem them; the bills themselves causing the precious metals to disappear. In 1714, a public bank was established, loaning bills on land security. These continued to sink in value, causing so much loss to the community. The bills were loaned on mortgage, with interest, and one-fifth part of the principal payable annually. When the time of payment arrived, the paper money having sunk below its nominal value, the creditors were obliged to pay a much larger amount of it, or sacrifice their estates in payment of the mortgages. It was attempted to relieve this state of things by extending the limits of payment, but this course served only to prolong this state of things. The most intelligent men of the time were ignorant of what are now deemed the first principles of banking.

The land bank of 1741, like that of 1714, loaned bills, taking real estate for security, but possessed no means of redeeming them. In 1749, specie was introduced from England, in payment of the provincial expenses in the expedition to Cape Breton. This, in a great degree, checked the evil.

In 1749, after having used their first meeting-house for twenty years, the town passed a vote for building a new house for public worship, and appropriated the sum of 300l. "new tenor," ($1000) for the purpose. The building committee were instructed to let out the job to some one man, who would do the work "cheapest and best." This house, which was demolished but a few years since, was located on the slope of the hill, a few rods to the southeast of the present

F

meeting-house, on the spot now occupied by the school-house last built
in the centre district.

The town voted 3*l*. 5*s*. 5*d*. "to pay for the Rum and other articles
used at the raising of the meeting-house," and "18*s*. 8*d*. to Josiah
Dodge for the use of his Rope," on the same occasion. The conduct
of the building committee, though they probably exerted themselves
to have the work done "cheapest and best," did not give satisfaction.
When they had expended the sum of 522*l*. it was not allowed to them
by the town; and a motion was made in town meeting to "proceed
against them in the steps of the laws," but this did not prevail. The
difficulty was afterwards adjusted, and the committee was paid.

Mr. Stearns continued to preach till his death, which occurred in
March, 1761. His funeral expenses were defrayed by the town.
They also voted to his brothers "weeds and gloves, to his sisters, veils,
handkerchiefs, gloves and fans, and to his sons-in-law, weeds and
gloves." The whole of Mr. Stearns' salary for 1761, was paid to
his widow.

The condition of the highways, in the early history of the town,
can hardly be imagined at the present time. For the most part they
were merely "bridle paths," winding through the woods, over one hill
after another, and making the travelled distance between two places
nearly double what it is now. Wheel carriages had not then been
introduced. Travelling was performed on horseback. In order that
people might not lose their direction, trees were marked on one side
of the way. A few roads, which would soon prove the destruction of
one of our modern carriages, were laid out at an early season, near to
the centre of the town. But in that part of the town which is now
Fitchburg, there was nothing of the kind, till, in 1743, a committee
was chosen "to lay out and mark a way to the west line of our town,
in order to answer the request of the Honorable Thomas Berry, Esqr.,
in behalf of Ipswich Canada, (Winchendon) and to accommodate
Dorchester Canada, (Ashburnham) and the new towns above us."
The two most important roads, which led from this part of the town
to the centre, were the one by David Page's (J. L. Haynes') and

corresponding nearly with what is now denominated the old road, and the one by David Goodridge's, who lived on the place now occupied by Wm. Bemis, near the brick factory at South Fitchburg.

In 1745 the town voted "that the men that live in the bounds of Maj. Hartwell's company build the bridge over the North Branch in the way that goes to David Goodridge's, and the bridge over the sd. North Branch in the way that goes to David Page's." At the same time, the men residing in the bounds of Capt. Willard's company were directed to build the bridge over "Mullepus Brook," in the northerly part of Lunenburg. The first of these bridges was where the arched bridge is in South Fitchburg, and the second near to where the stone mill is, in the "Old City." In 1748, the road was laid out from the "south side of Appletree Hill," over the bridge in the Old City, thence over the hill, and so on to Narrhagansett No. 2, (Westminster.)

The bridge near David Goodridge's was rebuilt in 1749, and at the same time a new one was built between James Poole's (where Joseph Farnsworth now lives) and Narrhagansett. This bridge was probably near Osborn's mills. In 1750, the selectmen were empowered *to cut away the trees* in the road to Dorchester Canada. At this time the annual expense of maintaining the highways was about equal to the salary of the minister, viz:—60*l.* "lawful ·money." It was afterwards increased by the necessary expenses of the roads in the westerly part of the town.

What little communication there was between Lunenburg and "the new towns above," was principally made through the road by David Page's, already mentioned. This road probably passed the village of Fitchburg, nearly in the same place with the present travelled way. It then wound up the hill by Enoch Caldwell's—over Flat rock— through the land lately owned by Sylvanus Lapham—and thence to what was then Lunenburg west line, and into Dorchester Canada. John Scott, who lived where Benj. Scott now resides, had been for a long time desirous of a more direct route to the centre of Lunenburg; but the town would not accede to his wishes. He accordingly procured a

Court's committee, who laid the present Scott road, "to the great satisfaction of Mr. John Scott," as the Records say. This road passed from the middle of Lunenburg by the log house where John Battles, Jr., now lives, then by Ebenezer Bridge's, where Deacon Jaquith now resides, and then by Scott's own house, and so on to the road before mentioned. This Scott road was for some years quite a celebrated thoroughfare, and used to be called the Crown Point road.

Who were the earliest settlers in the territory which now constitutes the town of Fitchburg, it is impossible to determine with accuracy. Enough has been said respecting David Page. John Scott, above mentioned, appears to have been residing on his farm in 1734—how much earlier I cannot tell. In this year was recorded the birth of his eldest son Edward. Jonathan Wood, who was a man of considerable note, was living on the place where Widow Grace Wood lately lived (the last house in Fitchburg previous to passing Baker's bridge,) in 1735, when the birth of his first child was recorded. It is probable that he had been living there for some time. Samuel Poole lived on Charles Beckwith's place before 1740, and his brother James Poole was living at the same time where Joseph Farnsworth now lives. David Goodridge, at quite an early period, commenced on his farm at South Fitchburg. His house was partly on, or very near to, the spot now occupied by the dwelling house of William Bemis. David Carlile lived where there is (or lately was) a cellar hole near to the bridge over Baker's brook, on the road leading to Isaiah Putnam's. Before 1745, Isaac Gibson was living where widow Prudence Gibson now resides, and his brother Reuben, where Arrington Gibson lives. Timothy Bancroft lived on the farm now owned by Joseph Marshall. Ephraim Whitney lived where Stephen Lowe now lives—Thomas Dutton on Capt. Benjamin Wheeler's place—William Henderson on Abel F. Adams' farm—John White on the French place, now occupied by William Wyman.

In the year 1745 or '6, Amos Kimball, and his cousin Ephraim moved from Bradford into this town. Amos built the house where Sam'l Hale now lives, and Ephraim the house on the Story farm. They probably owned land down to the river, and so up the same, including Rollstone. They built a gristmill with one run of stones, soon. after they came here, on the place where the stone factory now stands. The dam which they built is said to have been not more than forty feet in length, in consequence of a natural bank, on the south side of the river, confining the water to a narrow channel at this place. This dam was made of a log laid across the river, having "spoilings" driven in above it. Almost every year a freshet would sweep round the south end of the dam and oblige them to extend it several feet further.

The Kimballs, living at rather too great a distance to take immediate charge of their mill, they employed one Hodgkins for *tender*. He built for himself a little hut or stall on the ground between I. Phillips' store and the house below. This habitation of Hodgkins was the first building, with the exception of the mill, erected in what is now the Old City.

At this time Samuel Poole had a garrison—Capt. Samuel Hunt, who lived where David Page previously lived, had one—there was one at Isaac Gibson's, and one at Joseph Spafford's.

Between the years 1740 and 1750, the Indians did not cease to keep the inhabitants of the frontier towns,—and this town may fairly have been considered as such—in a state of constant alarm. England at this time was waging a war with France; and their colonists suffered dreadfully from the incursions and attacks of the savages, who were instigated by the French in Canada. The French government paid a large bounty for English scalps, and a still larger one for English prisoners. Prisoners were also ransomed for large sums of money, which was a further inducement to the Indians to save their prisoners alive. Though the war with France was closed by the treaty of Aix la Chapelle, in 1748, the dread of Indian depredations did not cease till several years after. Indian scouts were frequently reported to have been seen—alarms, many of which undoubtedly arose from false apprehensions, were excited—and fears were daily aroused from a consciousness of insecurity.

In the summer of 1747, a body of Indians made their appearance within the borders of this town, and committed several acts of depredation. As this was the only occasion, of which we have authentic accounts, that the Indians made their appearance in this town, as enemies, I have thought that it would not prove uninteresting to notice the incursion with some degree of particularity.

Besides the bounty paid in Canada for English prisoners, and the exposed condition of this settlement, another reason for the attack upon this place, as I have been informed, was the following :—

There was living at this time, in the neighborhood of Mr. John Fitch, who then resided upon a spot very near to the place where the brick house of Oliver Kendall stands, in Ashby, a certain half-tamed Indian, called Surdody. This part of Ashby was then included in Lunenburg. Mr. Fitch accidentally felled a tree, one day, onto the wigwam of Surdody, while the latter was absent on some hunting expedition. Surdody, on his return home at evening, found his dwelling crushed to the earth, and his wrath was kindled. Fitch did not seek him with an apology, or with any offer of reparation; neither did Surdody request any recompense of, or shower any reproaches upon his white neighbor. He sought a recompense more congenial with the Indian disposition. He immediately took up his line of march for the north, and soon laid his grievances before his copper-coloured brethren in Canada. He described to them the defenceless state of the whites in this region, and prevailed upon a band of them to accompany him back upon a laudable expedition of vengeance and booty.

Mr. Fitch, feeling insecure, had previously petitioned the government for assistance. Two soldiers, named Jennings and Blodgett, were accordingly stationed at his house, for his protection. Upon the arrival of the Indians, some of them posted themselves in lurking positions about Fitch's dwelling—a body of them passing over the hill where John Turner lives, to the hill where William Coggswell and Edmund Proctor live, and even to the south part of the town, to the hill where Stephen Houghton lives, lurked about in the thick woods there, to take a view of the state of things in Lunenburg. As it happened to be Sunday, and as our fathers were more in the habit of going to meeting than their descendants at the present day, the Indians were not a little surprised and disappointed at seeing such a concourse of white faces, and men armed for attack—for at that time people went armed to church. They accordingly skulked back to their comrades, telling them that the pale faces were as thick as the leaves in the forest, and that it was utterly hopeless to attack them there. But they determined not to go back empty-handed. So they killed an ox which was quietly browsing in the woods; made an encampment, roasted their beef, and made merry with one another. This camp was afterwards discovered in a field then belonging to John Scott, and is not a great distance from McIntire's saw-mill, on the Scott road. It was (if it is not now) called the camp pasture, from this circumstance.

Before making an attack upon John Fitch, they divided into parties, and reconnoitered the neighborhood. On the brow of Pearl Hill they anxiously looked down upon the Gibsons, and longed to lay their hands on them. But these giants, whose size and strength would have done honor to the days of chivalry, were hardy looking men, and to use the words of one of their descendants, "the Indians didn't dare to *tackle* them." In a kind of cave on the hill were afterwards found a gun barrel, an axe, and several implements of Indian manufacture—supposed to have been left here on this occasion.

They proceeded to David Goodridge's, one evening, and one of them, as he afterwards informed Mr. Fitch, when in captivity, climbed into a tree near to the house, for the purpose of reconnoitering the premises through the window.

He saw a white *squaw* feeding her papoose with milk. They retired from this house without doing any damage.

On the following day, Mr. Goodridge was out on horseback, in search of a cow, which did not return home the previous night. He was on the hill, near the place where S. Ward Harris now lives, when the Indians suddenly started up in the path, a few paces in front of him, and commanded him to surrender. He immediately turned his horse in order to retreat, when lo! another Indian, completely armed, faced him there to cut him off in that direction. He then made a circuit, aiming to come down the hill towards Kimball's mills. The savage ran in a direct line to cut him off in this direction also. It was a fair race, but the horseman gained upon the footman—and as Goodridge passed in front, the Indian, perceiving that it was in vain to thing of taking him alive, fired—but fortunately, owing to the rapidity of Goodridge's motion, or some other cause, missed his mark. The leaps of the horse down the steep part of the hill were afterwards measured, and found to be eighteen feet in length.

In his flight, Goodridge lost his hat, and the Indians secured it as a trophy. It is not a little remarkable that, about ten years after this, in the succeeding war, an Indian was taken somewhere on Connecticut river, having on his head the identical hat of Deacon David Goodridge, not much the worse for wear. On his getting clear of the Indians, Goodridge betook himself to Page's garrison, and an alarm was forthwith fired. In a short time men poured in from Lunenburg, and even from Groton. It is worthy of notice that in two hours after the alarm was given, a Major Willard, with a company of cavalry, arrived at the garrison from Lancaster.

The Indians, upon the alarm being given, retired to the top of Rollstone, from whence they could command a view of the movements beneath them, and seeing a great commotion, and people flocking in from abroad, they thought it advisable to withdraw into some secret place.

It was on the following morning, according to the accounts of aged people, that the garrison of John Fitch was attacked. He lived at this time several miles distant from his nearest neighbors, and was the farthest west of them all. His family consisted of himself, wife, four children, (one son and three daughters,) and the two soldiers already mentioned. One of these, on going out of the fort to examine about the premises, (thinking from certain indications that Indians were lurking in the vicinity) was immediately shot down.

The Indians then commenced the attack upon the garrison, which Fitch and the remaining soldier defended for a short time. The latter was soon shot through the port hole, and Fitch was induced to surrender. Surdody was desirous of having him killed on the spot, but he was overruled in this by the others, who were disposed to carry him and his family into captivity, and so receive the highest bounty from the French, and a large sum for their ransom. Fitch, accompanied by his wife and four children, and under the escort of his captors, was carried to Montreal. His habitation was at such a distance from the principal settlement, that the report of his capture was not spread till the following morning. It reached the middle of Lunenburg, however, long before the rising of the sun, and the alarm, (three muskets, heavily loaded, discharged with a certain interval between each report) was immediately fired. Soldiers arrived in an incredibly short period, from Groton, Lancaster, and even from Westford. They immediately put themselves under the command of Major Hartwell, and started in pursuit. They had not proceeded far beyond the smoking ruins of the garrison, before they discovered a paper stuck in the bark of a tree. This contained a request, signed by Fitch, not to have his friends pursue him; for the Indians had given him to understand what his destiny was to be if they were not molested; but if they should be pursued, and likely to be overtaken, then they should forthwith kill him, together with his wife and children. The soldiers, on the receipt of this, returned. Fitch and his family were carried to Montreal, where they remained for about one year, enduring great hardships. They were then ransomed, principally by means of a subscription raised among the people of Bradford, the place of his former residence. They all lived to return to their home, with the exception of Mrs. Fitch, who died while on her return, at Providence, R. I.*

After this period, Mr. Fitch was prospered in his worldly concerns, and became one of the wealthiest men of the place. When the country above him became settled, he opened a public house. He presents one of many instances of the uncertainty of riches. He lived to the good old age of *one hundred and five* years, and died in the poor-house of Ashby!

A few Indians remained behind, after the capture of Fitch, to observe its effects. They continued several days skulking about, and on the watch for more prisoners, or scalps. Deacon Amos Kimball was hoeing corn in his field, and, hearing a rustling in the brush fence near him, he looked in that direction and saw a gun pointed at him through the fence, by an Indian. The latter seemed to be reserving his fire till his victim should draw a little nearer. Kimball knew that if he ran, it would be sure death, as he was then so near; so he pretended not to see anything, and kept scratching with his hoe, and working off—looking down, as if busily at work—till he supposed that he had attained to a sufficient distance to give him

---

*I would here correct an error in Whitney's account of this affair, which is as follows :—"In the summer of the year 1749, the Indians came into the northwest limits of the town, and killed two soldiers, Jennings and Blodget, who were stationed there, and carried Mr. John Fitch and his family into captivity, who all returned in safety, after enduring incredible hardships and fatigues, except Mrs. Fitch, who sickened and died in Canada."

There is an error of two years in this statement. In the first place, the war between France and England was concluded in 1748, and the French would not pay a bounty for English prisoners after that period. Secondly, an aged man of this town, recently deceased, remembered how old he was when Fitch was taken, and was quite positive that the event occurred on the 16th of July, 1747. Thirdly, the Records of Lunenburg state that Susanna Fitch ye wife of Mr. John Fitch Deceast December ye 24th 1748, at Providence in ye Collony of Rhod Island." Now Mrs. Fitch could not die at Providence in 1748, and be taken captive by the Indians in the following summer. The authority of the Records cannot be disputed. Furthermore, the intentions of marriage between Mr. Fitch and his second wife were recorded in Dec. 1750—quite too early if he was taken in 1749, and his first wife lived nearly or quite a year after the event.

There is a story current, respecting this second wife of John Fitch, to this effect:—She undertook, one day, to make some candles, and accordingly put the *ingredients*—tallow and wicking—together in a kettle over the fire, and commenced stirring them together. This she continued to do till she was reduced nearly to the state of the liquid over which she was engaged. One of her neighbors enquiring the meaning of such unusual conduct, she replied that she was making candles, and wondered very much " why they did not *come!* "

Jacob Fitch, who was an infant when he was carried into Canada, was afterwards a clerk in the store of Dr. John Taylor in Lunenburg. Though in other respects well formed, his lower limbs were of dwarfish size, in consequence of the rigor with which he was bound.

a chance to escape. He then made good use of his heels. The Indian, as his only chance, fired, and the ball struck a tree a short distance in front of his intended victim. As Kimball immediately gave the alarm, this scout thought it best to be off. A few of them made a circuit through Westminster—killed one man named Bowman, who was at work in a field, and, according to the statement of my informant, (Arrington Gibson) "carried his scalp into captivity"—then passed rapidly on towards Canada, and overtook their companions with Fitch, before their arrival at Montreal. This was the last of Indian warfare and depredations within our borders.

After the events above detailed, and previous to the incorporation of the town of Fitchburg, several families moved into the westerly part of Lunenburg, whose names will be given when I speak of those living in Fitchburg when it was erected into a separate town. Capt. Samuel Hunt came into this town (from Worcester, as I have been told) and built a part of the house now occupied by James L. Haynes. In the year 1761, he commenced keeping tavern there. This was the first public house ever kept in the precincts of Fitchburg.

At this period, considerable difficulty was experienced in the collection of taxes. The paper money was of uncertain value, and the constables, upon whom this duty devolved, had not sufficient authority to enforce prompt payments. They were required to pay over the sums which they had been ordered to collect, within a certain period; and if they failed to collect them, the loss fell upon their own shoulders. It was not uncommon for them to pay their fines, rather than accept office. In Jan. 1763, a town meeting was held in "Capt. Joshua Hutchens' Long Chamber," when Abijah Hovey was chosen constable. He being absent, a messenger was despatched for him, who reported "that Mr. Hovey would not serve the town as constable,—would be glad if the town would excuse him; if they would not, he would pay the fine." And so he paid his fine. "Then chose Jonathan Pearce constable. He replied that he did not choose to serve, unless he could be sufficiently authorised to collect the taxes. After a long disputation and debate, Mr. Pearce was again desired to declare to the town his acceptance or non-acceptance of the office. He desired more time for consideration; and finally refused to serve." Jonathan Bradstreet was then chosen. "Mr. Bradstreet being immediately notified of the town's choice, presented himself to the town, and being asked by the moderator whether he would accept the office of a constable, Mr. Bradstreet replied that he *scrupled* whether the fine could be recovered of him ; the moderator insisting upon a peremptory answer, he replied he *scrupled* whether the fine could be recovered of him,"—and finally he refused to serve. Richard Taylor was next chosen, "who made his appearance, and declared he would not serve once and again." The town *excused* him. Paul Wetherbee was then chosen, who accepted the office.

I have already mentioned the death of Rev. Mr. Stearns, the second minister of Lunenburg, which took place in March, 1761, in the 52d year of his age, and 28th of his ministry. He was much beloved by his people, who built a monument to his memory.* They also paid the whole amount of his salary for the year 1761 to his widow, "Madam Ruth Stearns."

---

*The following is a copy of the inscription upon the tomb-stone of Rev. Mr. Stearns :—

" THIS MONUMENT,
ERECTED BY THE TOWN OF LUNENBURGH,
IS SACRED TO THE MEMORY
OF THE REVEREND DAVID STEARNS
THEIR MUCH BELOVED AND RESPECTED PASTOR,
WHO DEPARTED THIS LIFE
IN THE JOYFUL EXPECTATION OF A BETTER
ON THE 9TH DAY OF MARGH A. D. 1761
AND IN THE 52d. YEAR OF HIS AGE.
IN HIS PRIVATE CAPACITY
HE WAS A KIND HUSBAND, A TENDER PARENT
AN AFFECTIONATE BROTHER AND A FAITHFUL FRIEND.
IN HIS MINISTERIAL CHARACTER
HIS CONVERSATION WAS PURE ENTERTAINING
AND INSTRUCTIVE
HIS DOCTRINES PLAIN AND SCRIPTURAL
AND HIS LIFE TRULY EXEMPLARY.

He was adorned
with hospitality, with singular prudence and a most endearing benevolence; with a good knowledge of men and things, with a fervent zeal for the Glory of Christ, and the salvation of souls; and was governed by the influence of these accomplishments.   Help, Lord, for the Godly man ceaseth."

Immediately after the decease of Mr. Stearns, Rev. Josiah Bridge. (Harvard University, 1758) was hired to preach; and in August of the same year, Rev. Samuel Payson, a class-mate of Mr. Bridge, was hired. In the following February, the town " gave him a call," offering him an annual salary of 80*l*., and 200*l*. " for his encouragement and comfortable settlement." He was ordained in Sept., 1762. A committee was chosen " to make suitable provision for the venerable Council, and other gentlemen of note and distinction who shall attend the ordination."

Mr. Payson continued but five months in the ministry, having died in February, 1763, aged 24. He was a native of Walpole, Mass.* Rev. Ebenezer Sparhawk, of Templeton, was invited " to come and pray with the town," and the neighboring ministers were invited to attend the funeral. The town also " voted to give to Miss Elizabeth Stearns, (affianced to Rev. Mr. Payson) a neat, handsome suit of mourning,"—" to the father and brothers of the deceased, weeds and gloves—to his mother and half sister, veils, handkerchiefs and gloves."

Rev. Messrs. Champney, Fiske and Davis were hired to preach after Mr. Stearns' death. Mr. Davis received an invitation to

---

*The inscription upon the tomb-stone of Rev. Mr. Payson is as follows:—

" QUIESCUNT
SUB HOC TUMULO
RELIQUIÆ
REV. SAMUELIS PAYSON A. M.
QUI
ECCLESIÆ LUNENBURGENSIS PASTOR
DOCTUS FIDELIS
PRÆSTANTI VIR INGENIO
MORUMQUE GESTU AMABILI
VIRTUTIS POTIUSQUAM DIERUM PLENUS
ATROPHÆ MORBO
OCCUBUIT
ID. FEB. SALUT, M. DCCLXIII,
ÆT. XXIV.
A FATHER
ERECTS THIS MONUMENT
TO THE MEMORY OF A BELOVED SON."

It may be translated thus:

Here rest, within this tomb, the remains of Rev. Samuel Payson A. M. the learned and exemplary Pastor of the church of Lunenburg. He was a man of superior abilities, and of an amiable disposition; more distinguished for virtues than for length of days. He died of an atrophy in February A. D. 1763, aged 24.

"settle," which he declined. May 19th, the town concurred with
the church in appointing "a fast on Thursday come fortnight."
In November, Rev. Zabdiel Adams was procured to preach. He
was settled soon after Fitchburg was incorporated.

For several years previous to this event, (the incorporation of
the town) the inhabitants of the westerly part of Lunenburg began
to have shrewd suspicions that they were able to walk alone—that
they were sufficient in knowledge and numbers to manage their
own affairs—and that it was an unnecessary burthen upon them
to be compelled to travel the distance of five or ten miles to attend Divine service, and transact the ordinary business of town
affairs.

It will be seen, upon an inspection of the case, that there
was a pretty good foundation for these opinions. By an examination of the Records, it will be seen that a very fair proportion of those who were selected to manage the most important affairs of the town, was taken from among those afterwards belonging to Fitchburg. It ought furthermore to be considered, that a ride of ten miles then, was quite a different
affair from a ride of that distance now. Of the roads at that
period, mention has already been made. They were but little
better than cow-paths. When this town was incorporated, there
were no wheel carriages here of a higher rank than ox carts.
Any vehicle of lighter construction would have soon gone to destruction over such roads. Journeys were then made on horseback
or on foot. A spruce young gentleman, in treating the mistress
of his affections to a ride—or the sober-minded husband in carrying the partner of his life to church—brings the sure-paced animal
to the horse-block, and mounts—the lady places herself on the
pillion behind him. The horse starts off on a walk,—the greatest speed at which it would be considered safe to drive him,
through roads so rough. They thus pursue their journey, winding along up one hill, and then another. The horse leaps over
the smaller streams, for fear of wetting his feet, and wades boldly

through the larger ones, even to endangering the feet of his riders. Now the gentleman dismounts to "let down" the bars, and then proceeds along, dodging under the boughs, twigs and limbs of trees. He must start very early, or arrive at his journey's end very late. It is therefore not to be wondered at that the early settlers of this town began so early as they did, to desire a separation from the parent stock, that they might be nearer home in the performance of their public duties, whether they were such as they owed to the community, or to their Maker.

From the record of the town meeting, March, 1757, it appears that Samuel Hunt and others petitioned to the town of Lunenburg, to have the westerly part of the same set off, in order to have it incorporated into a separate town. This petition was referred to a committee, with directions to report at the next May meeting. At the May meeting, the committee reported—but whether in accordance with the prayer of the petitioners or not, we are not informed. The report, however, excited considerable debate, and was recommitted for an amendment —and the committee was directed to report at the following September meeting. Among the recorded proceedings of the September meeting, not one word is said respecting the report, or Samuel Hunt's petition. Nothing further respecting this subject is recorded, till May, 1761, when the town voted that the request of Samuel Hunt and others " be so far granted that *one-half* of the land in the township of Lunenburg, and the westerly part thereof—running a parallel line with the west line of said township—be and hereby is set off a separate *Parish* by itself; Provided they shall place their meeting-house as near the *centure* of said parish as may be, so as to accommodate the whole, and that as soon as they are able and do maintain the Gospel among themselves, that they shall be freed from all costs and charges of maintaining the Gospel in the first parish." But this grant did not satisfy the petitioners ; for the record states that immediately a motion was made that the request be granted in full— which passed in the negative.

In the following August, the request of Amos Kimball and others, to be set off into a separate town, was presented. It shared the same fate with that of Samuel Hunt—with the exception that it did not live nearly so long, for it was killed on the spot. "After debate thereon, it passed in the negative."

In the warrant for town meeting in March, 1763, there was an article, to hear the petition of Dea. Benjamin Foster and nine others, "to set off into a district and precinct by themselves" all the inhabitants on the westerly side of Pearl Hill brook and Dorchester farm, so called. The town refused to act on this article.

In the warrant for town meeting in the May following, there was an article of similar import—with the exception that it said, "To see if the town will consent that application may be made to the General Court, to incorporate the westerly part, &c., into a town. This article was negatived. But the advocates for this measure made another attempt in the following January, and with much better success, for the town then voted to "let the people go." This vote was passed January 25th, 1764, at "the request of Dea. Benjamin Foster, Dea. Samuel Putnam, and others," which was as follows: — That the town vote "the lands in said Lunenburg which lie west and westwardly of the line hereafter described, should be set off from said town, that so the said lands, and inhabitants thereon, may be formed by the General Court into a town or district, as they shall think proper." (Here follows a description of the line, which corresponds with the easterly boundary of Fitchburg.) This was granted on condition that "the inhabitants should pay their minister's tax, as heretofore they had done, until they should be formed into a district."

The long sought-for object of the people of the westerly part of Lunenburg having been obtained, a committee consisting of Messrs. John Fitch, Amos Kimball, Samuel Hunt, Ephraim Whitney, and Jonathan Wood, was chosen to wait upon the

General Court, to procure the act of incorporation; and they performed their duty so promptly and perseveringly, that on the 3d of February, 1764,—just nine days after the passage of the above vote—the act passed the Legislature, and received the signature of the Governor.

February 3d, 1764, was therefore the BIRTH-DAY OF FITCHBURG, which was 72 years old on the 3d day of February, 1836.

It is the general report that the town was named in honor of John Fitch, who was the first man on the committee appointed to procure the act of incorporation, and was the same individual taken captive by the Indians in 1747. Some people think that the town was named in honor of a Col. Timothy Fitch, a wealthy merchant of Boston, who owned extensive tracts of land in the town, and was considered, in those days, as a man of "note and distinction." It is true that John Fitch, at this time, was an extensive landholder, and perhaps a man of some influence—and he may have taken an active part in getting the town incorporated. Yet there were many in the town who were held in higher estimation than he. Previous to this period, he seems to have been elected to only three offices by the good people of Lunenburg. In 1738, he was chosen one of the "Hogge rieves;" afterwards he was chosen "to take care of Deer," and again "to take care of fire and burn the woods." These certainly were not distinguished stations. But whether the town was named in honor of this individual, or of the above named Col. Fitch, is a point which will probably remain forever in obscurity. This is a circumstance not a little surprising, when it is considered how recently the town received its name, and that there are people now living who remember the event perfectly well.

The act of incorporation, which the committee was so prompt in procuring, is as follows :—

"Anno regni Regis Georgii tertii Quarto.

Be it enacted by the Governor, Council and House of Repre-

sentatives, That the inhabitants, with their lands, in the westerly part of Lunenburg—beginning," &c. (Here follows the boundaries of the town by "stakes and stones," which it is not necessary to repeat) "be and hereby are set off and erected into a separate town, by the name of Fitchburgh; and that said town be invested with all the powers, privileges, and immunities that other towns in this Province do, or may, by law, enjoy;—that of sending a Representative to the General Assembly only excepted;—and that the inhabitants of said town shall have full power and right, from time to time, to join with the said town of Lunenburg in the choice of a Representative or Representatives, and be subject to pay their proportionable part of the charges, who may be chosen either in the town of Lunenburg, or in the town of Fitchburgh, in which choice they shall enjoy all the privileges which by law 'they would have been entitled to if this act had not been made; and the Selectmen of the town of Lunenburg shall issue their warrant to one or more of the constables of Fitchburgh, requiring them to notify the inhabitants of the town of Fitchburgh of the time and place of meeting for such choice; *Provided*, nevertheless, *And be it further enacted*, that the said town of Fitchburgh shall pay their proportion of all town, county, and Province taxes, already set on, or granted to be raised by, said town of Lunenburg, as if this act had not been made;—

And be it further enacted—That Edward Hartwell, Esq., be, and hereby is empowered to issue his warrant directed to some principal inhabitant of said town of Fitchburgh, requiring him to notify and warn the inhabitants of said town, qualified by law to vote in town affairs, to meet at such time and place as shall therein be set forth, to choose all such officers as shall be necessary to manage the affairs of said town."

This bill passed the House Feb. 2d, 1764, and the Council on the following day—when it also received the assent of the Governor.

At this period there were in the whole town not more than forty-three or four families, and the whole number of inhabitants did not much, if any, exceed two hundred and fifty.* At the present time it contains more than ten times that number.

Perhaps a more accurate picture of the town in 1764, could not be presented, than by stating the place of residence of each family living in the town when it was incorporated. Considerable pains have been taken to make this statement correct.

Amos Kimball† lived where Samuel Hale now lives.

Ephraim Kimball lived where the Storeys now live.

Samuel Pierce and William Steward lived where Capt. James Cowdin and Jacob Tollman now live.

Solomon Steward‡ lived where there is a cellar hole, and a barn lately stood, on the farm now owned by O. H. Fox.

Phinehas Steward lived where the " Poor House" now stands.

Robert (?) Wares lived where Joseph Battles now lives.

Samuel Poole lived where Charles Beckwith now lives.

James Poole lived where Joseph Farnsworth now lives.

Kendall Boutelle lived where Capt. A. Boutelle now lives.

Francis Fullam lived where Jacob Fullam now lives.

Silas Snow lived where William Downe now lives.

Nehemiah Fuller lived where Thomas B. Goodhue now lives.

Ephraim Osborne lived where Joseph Downe, Esq. now lives.

Hezekiah Hodgkins lived where Benjamin Whitney now lives.

James Leach (Litch?) lived where P. Williams Esq. now lives.

Abraham Smith lived where Daniel Works now lives.

---

*To the brief account of Fitchburg in an old edition of Morse's Gazetteer, some unknown person has appended a manuscript note, stating that the population of the town, in 1765, was 259. What degree of credit this statement is entitled to, I know not.

†He was a man of unblemished reputation, and was always highly esteemed by his fellow citizens. He died in 1774, at the age of 57. None of his descendants now remain in the town. George Kimball Esqr. of Lunenburg, who built the house where Jacob Caldwell now resides, was a brother of Amos.

‡Martha, wife of Solomon Steward, died in 1777. She was buried in the lower grave yard at Lunenburg. Her grave stone declares that " She Was a Vartus Wife a Kind Neighbour & a Tender Parent.

Mournfull Children Hear I Lay
as You are Now So Once Was I
as I am Now So You Must be
Prepare Your Selves to Follow Me."

Charles Willard lived where Adin H. Hammond now lives.

Edward Scott lived where Joseph T. Scott now lives.

Ebenezer Bridge lived where Dea. Jacob Jaquith now lives.

Ezra Whitney lived where Daniel Lowe now loves.

Reuben Gibson lived where Arrington Gibson now lives.

Isaac Gibson* lived where Widow P. Gibson now lives.

William Chadwick lived near to, and a little north of where John Hapgood now lives.

Nich. Danforth lived in the pasture nearly opposite I. Putnam's.

Isaiah Witt lived where Isaiah Putnam now lives.

Thomas Gerry lived where Joseph Fairbanks now lives.

Joseph Spafford lived in the log house where John Battles, Jr., now lives.

Ephraim Whitney lived where Stephen Lowe now lives.

John White lived where William Wyman now lives.

Timothy Bancroft lived where Joseph Marshall now lives.

Thomas Damary lived where there is a tan yard, near to Nathan Battles'.

Jesse French lived where Jacob H. Merriam now lives.

Thomas Dutton lived where Capt. Benjamin Wheeler now lives.

William Henderson† lived where Abel F. Adams now lives.

Samuel Hunt lived where James L. Haynes now lives.

Timothy Parker lived in the *garrison* house, formerly D. Page's.

Jonathan Wood lived where John Younglove now lives.

David Goodridge lived where William Bemis now lives.

Jonathan Holt lived opposite the house of Avery Stockwell.

---

*The personal prowess of these Gibsons was quite proverbial. On one occasion, Isaac Gibson, in his rambles on Pearl Hill found a bear's cub, which he immediately seized as his legitimate prize. The mother of the cub came to the rescue of her offspring. Gibson retreated, and the bear attacked him in the rear, to the manifest detriment of his pantaloons. This finally compelled him to face his unwelcome antagonist, and they closed in a more than fraternal embrace. Gibson, being the more skilful wrestler of the two, "threw" bruin, and they came to the ground together. Without relinquishing the hug both man and beast now rolled over each other to a considerable distance down the hill, receiving sundry bruises by the way. When they reached the bottom, both were willing to relinquish the contest, without any further experience of each other's prowess. It was a drawn game—the bear losing her cub, and Gibson his pantaloons.

†He was a half crazy Irishman, and went to Colraine soon after the incorporation of Fitchburg. In about ten years he returned in poverty, and involved Fitchburg and Lunenburg in a law-suit respecting his maintenance.

Samuel Hodgkins lived a little to the south of the old city store.
Samuel Walker lived where C. Marshall now lives.

Phinehas Goodell lived in the south-westerly part of the town. His place of residence in not exactly known.

The above mentioned individuals and their families, composed the population of Fitchburg. Their dwellings, in almost every instance, were far apart—here and there a house, scattered over a large territory. A single dwelling house stood in the " Old City," and in the village, where the population is now so thickly clustered together, not a single house was erected. The winds which swept down the valley of the Nashua, sighed through the pines which here formed a dense forest.

Within the first few years after the incorporation of the town, several new families selected it as their place of residence. It would be tedious to enumerate all these new comers ; but there is one who, by the influence which he exerted over the affairs of the town in its infancy, by the character which he helped to give it, and by the high estimation in which he seems to have been held, merits a more particular notice.

Thomas Cowdin, Esq. moved into Fitchburg in the July following its incorporation. He appears to have been one of those persons who, without the advantages of birth, education or fortune, unaided by the influence of patronage or favor, but relying solely upon the energies of a sound intellect and active mind, frequently elevate themselves to a rank above their neighbors.

He was born in Stow, in 1720, and went as an apprentice to the blacksmith's trade, to Marlborough, where he served his time. He then removed to Worcester, and commenced his business on the main street. He belonged to a company of cavalry in that town. Several years previous to the old French War— as it is called—but at a time when the Indians were exceedingly troublesome, he was pressed into the service, and marched up to Charlestown No. 4, under the command of one Captain Stevens. Here it was his fortune to encounter some dangers, and make some hair-breadth escapes from the savages. He was, on one occasion, selected to convey some despatches from that place to Fort Dummer. He buckled them in his knapsack, and, accompanied by two other soldiers, commenced his dangerous journey. They had not proceeded many miles when, on coming to the brow of a rather abrupt precipice, they looked down and beheld a very interesting group of savages. The latter perceived Cowdin and his associates at the same instant, and sounded the war-whoop in pursuit. As they were obliged to make some little circuit before they could climb the precipice, the whites improved the opportunity to get the start. Each of the three wisely took a different direction. Cowdin showed the red men a light pair of heels, and escaped by dint of running. One of his comrades took a "bee line" for Charlestown, where he arrived in safety, and gave the information that Cowdin and his despatches were probably taken. The third, being slow of foot, finding it impossible to escape his pursuers by running, crawled into some high grass before they came in sight, and thus escaped unnoticed. Cowdin bent his course for Ashuelot, (now Keene) where he arrived unharmed. From thence a company of soldiers was sent with him to Fort Dummer, where he delivered his despatches. On his return to Charlestown, he met companies which had been sent in pursuit of him; and other despatches of the same tenor had been sent forward to Fort Dummer, upon the presumption that he had been taken and slain.

While he was at Charlestown, he was one of a detachment of thirty men which was sent out to scour the woods of the neighborhood, to see if any Indians were lurking in that quarter. In this detachment was also the famous Chamberlain, who distinguished himself in that most bloody battle with the Indians, known as Lovell's fight, by killing with his own hands the Indian chief, Paugus.

Chamberlain had a dog with him, which had been nurtured in Indian wars. He could "scent" an Indian as far as a common dog could a pole-cat. In this ramble the dog came speedily in to his master. Chamberlain looked in his face and read his intelligence. "Stop," says he, "my dog says the red skins are near." They halted, and in a moment they heard the sound of an arrow whizzing by their heads. They look about, and Chamberlain soon discovers the lurking foe. He fired, and in a moment the Indians in large numbers, rose around them and fired. The whites charged upon them, and they fled. The scouring party returned to the fort, having a few of their number wounded.

Cowdin, in the capacity of sergeant, was at the siege and capture of Louisburg, and faced the enemy in the hottest of the fight, when the place was attacked in 1745.

When the war broke out between England and France, in 1755, Cowdin enlisted as ensign; and in that year he was engaged in the expedition against Nova Scotia. He served seven years during this war, and rose to the post of captain. Two of these years he was employed in this state, for the double purpose of forwarding invalids, when they had sufficiently recovered to join the army, and for arresting deserters.

While engaged in this latter capacity, an incident occurred which serves very well to illustrate his determined perseverance. He had intimation of a certain deserter, who was making his way towards the state of New York. He started in pursuit of the fugitive, and finally burrowed him—so to speak—one Sunday morning, in a Dutch meeting-house. It was during divine service; but Cowdin rushed in and seized upon him. A scuffle ensued, much to the amazement of the sedate congregation. The fellow attempted to kill his captor, but Cowdin succeeded in overpowering and binding him. He then brought his prisoner from New York to Boston, for the purpose of putting him into the castle; but on his arrival there, it was ascertained that the soldier had last deserted from Crown Point, and therefore Cowdin was ordered to convoy him to the latter place.

This journey through the wilderness he accomplished alone with his prisoner, who very well knew that death would be his portion when delivered over to the proper tribunal. At Crown Point the prisoner was recognized as a man who had enlisted and deserted, in a short space, no less than thirteen times. He was conveyed to Montreal, and shot.

Such circumstances as these serve better, perhaps, than other means, to set forth in its true light, the character of one of the early pioneers, who, from the period when he made this town his residence, to his death in 1792, took the lead in its public affairs.

When Cowdin came into this town, he purchased the tavern stand of Samuel Hunt, who thereupon removed to Worcester. Cowdin continued to keep a public house here (J. L. Haynes') for about ten years, when he removed to the Boutelle house, so called, in the Old City, which has lately been taken down.

He owned a great portion of the land included between the two roads leading to Lunenburg and Baker's brook. He also owned a tract on the westerly side of the road leading from his then dwelling house to Kimball's mills in the Old City. The first meeting-house built in Fitchburg, was placed on land given by him, and which was then called his wheat field. This meeting-house was nearly on the spot now covered by the brick school-house.

I have already mentioned the condition of the village at that period. It was covered by a forest. After leaving Jesse French's house and Kimball's mills, there was not a single dwelling house before arriving at Leach's, where P. Williams, Esqr., now lives. The pitch pine trees afforded an excellent shelter for deer, partridges and wild turkeys. David Boutelle's "muster field" was covered with a beautiful growth of white pine timber, which was not cut down till 1775, when Thomas Cowdin built a large addition to the Boutelle house, and opened it as a public house.

A Judge Oliver, of Salem, owned a range of lots, commencing on Cowdin's land, near the Fox house, so called, and thence extending on the river to where Phillips' brook unites with the Nashua. This tract embraced the whole of the village and Crockersville. He also owned a tract a mile square on Dean hill, so called, in the westerly part of the town. Judge Oliver or his heirs sold both of these tracts to one Elias Haskell, who came into this town, and built the house now owned by Capt. Dean.

This Haskell, by selling lots and loaning his money, was reputed to be very rich; but he was doomed to experience a reverse of fortune. He was compelled to receive his pay in the pernicious paper currency of the times, which depreciated so rapidly that it soon came to be but little better than so much brown paper. He afterwards purchased a small sandy farm in the north-easterly part of Lancaster, where he lived some years, and died in poverty.

Col. William Brown and Burnet Brown, the one belonging to Salem, the other to the south, owned a large tract of land in the region of where Levi Farwell now resides. In the westerly part of the town they owned another tract, a part of which is now included in the Hilton and Sheldon farms. Another tract was owned by them in the northerly part of the town.

In the south-westerly part, several hundred acres were given to the committee appointed by the General Court to allot the original proprietorships. This committee, it will be recollected, consisted of William Taylor, Samuel Thaxter, Francis Fullam, John Shipley, and Benjamin Whittemore. The land owned by Col. Timothy Fitch, was in the southerly part of the town.

On the 5th day of March, 1764, the first meeting which the town ever held in its corporate capacity, was called, according to the act of incorporation, by virtue of a warrant issued by Edward Hartwell, Esq., of Lunenburg, directed to Amos Kimball, one of the Constables of Fitchburg. It was held in the tavern of Capt. Samuel Hunt. Amos Kimball was moderator of this meeting, and Ephraim Whitney was chosen town clerk. Amos Kimball, David Goodridge, Samuel Hunt, Ephraim Whitney, and Reuben Gibson, were chosen selectmen.

In September following, at a town meeting, it was voted that " two miles on the westerly line of said town, beginning at the north-west corner, and half a mile on the easterly line, beginning at the north-east corner, on Townsend line, then running a straight line from one of these distances to the other, be set off to Mr. John Fitch and others, in order for them to join a part of Townsend and a part of Dorchester Canada, in order to make a Town, or Parish among themselves." This was giving away a large *slice* from the northern part of the town ; and the liberal conduct of the people of Fitchburg is contrasted favorably with that of the people of Lunenburg, in the affair of the incorporation of this town. Notwithstanding the willingness of Fitchburg to gratify Mr. Fitch in this respect, Ashby was not incorporated till three years afterwards, viz : in 1767.

In October, 1764, a committee was chosen on the part of this town, to confer with those of Lunenburg, Groton, and other towns, for petitioning the Great and General Court for a new county to be formed of several towns in the counties of Middlesex and Worcester. Several attempts had been made, in years previous, to attain this object, but they were always unsuccessful. The attempt now made shared the fate of the others. At this period, though the amount of business which the people of Fitchburg had to transact at the shire town was but little, compared with it now, they felt great inconvenience in being compelled to travel the distance of twenty-five miles to have a deed recorded, or to transact any other county business.

Until this time there had been no burying yard in the precincts of Fitchburg. The dead were carried the distance of nearly seven miles to Lunenburg. The first " grave yard " in Fitchburg was purchased near to their meeting-house, on the hill a little in the rear of the brick school-house, in the Old City. But few bodies were ever deposited here, in consequence of ledges of rock and other obstructions in the soil. In 1766 Dea. Amos Kimball, in consideration of the love and respect which he bore to the people of Fitchburg, gave to them one acre of land, on the southerly side of the river between the bridge and his house. The bodies buried in the first burying-place were exhumed, and re-interred in the new yard.

In November the town voted to have six weeks preaching, and directed their committee to apply to Rev. Peter Whitney, who accordingly came and preached in the tavern of Thomas Cowdin. The people of those days were less scrupulous in regard to the place where they met for public worship, than we, of the 19th century are ; a tavern then was no better than a tavern now, but *they* probably thought that their Maker regarded more the feelings with which his creatures offered up their petitions and adorations than the place in which they assembled for this purpose.

At the same meeting in November they voted to proceed to build a meeting-house. Their manner of proceeding in this affair was quite different from that usually pursued now; for the town determined to find the " stuff," and then employ people to work on the house, and finish a part at a time. Their first step was to get the frame raised and covered with rough boards; afterwards the lower floor was laid, then the outside was "finished ;" a place was made " for the minister to preach in," the pew ground was " dignified," and the house was " seated." Then galleries, and stairs leading to the same, were to be made, the house was " glassed " and finally " coloured." The town employed different persons to perform these jobs, which were . not all completed till the lapse of several years. The town was thinly peopled, and money was by no means plenty. The sum of 50*l.* ($166.66,) was voted to begin the house, which, built piece-meal, and with such slender means, would make but a sorry appearance in comparison with our modern temples. The people were obliged to act with rigid economy. Fortunes were not made in a day, and the expenses of maintaining the minister, and keeping the high-ways in repair, bore heavily upon a population whose income was very limited. They thought

it best to build no more at a time than they could pay for,
and to humble themselves a little, as they arranged themselves
on temporary seats around their preacher—and so proceed with
the work of building as their means allowed. Such a course was
preferable to that which is sometimes adopted in these latter
days — of erecting a splendid edifice at once, contracting a large
debt to pay for it, and then to be able barely to pay, year after
year, the interest, and perhaps a small portion of the principal.

Although the people of Fitchburg thus early manifested a proper
spirit in supporting the public institutions of religion, and doing
other things for the prosperity of the town, it must be acknowledged that they did not exhibit that zeal in the cause of education which its importance demanded, and which might be reason-
ably expected from them. During the first year of its incorporation,
it does not appear that there was any school in the town. In
1765, it was voted that two schools should be kept in the town
during the ensuing winter, and the sum of three pounds ($10)
was appropriated to this purpose. Mr. John Fitch and Dea.
Kendall Boutelle, who lived in the northern and southern extremi-
ties of the town, were exempted from any portion of this tax,
and had permission to establish schools among themselves. How
much benefit to the town was derived from two schools, each
drawing from the treasury the paltry sum of five dollars for the
pay of the teacher and all incidental expenses, I cannot pretend
to say. Incidental expenses, however, were but trifling. There
were no school-houses in the town; but the dwelling-houses of
individuals, who had vacant rooms that would answer for this
purpose, were freely offered for the public good. A school was
"kept" for some time in Wm. Chadwick's "corn-barn." The
"master" boarded in the several families of the district, which
bore the burthen or honor of his presence, for a stated number
of weeks, in rotation. The people also furnished fuel gratuitously;
and it is probable that the teacher received nearly the whole
amount of the money raised by the town.

In the succeeding year a more magnanimous disposition was manifested. The sum of 8*l.* ($26.66) was voted for the support of the schools—and this was the standing sum appropriated for the purpose for a considerable number of years. During the same time they were paying to their minister annually the sum of $200, or $300 (in addition to his 30 cords of wood)—eight times the amount which they paid for the education of their children. At the present time, the amount of money paid by the people for instruction, is just about equal to that paid to all the ministers in the town. It is but just to add that, previous to the incorporation of Fitchburg, Lunenburg appropriated a handsome sum to purposes of education.*

There were some peculiarities exhibited in the conduct of the fathers of this town, which savored strongly of their puritan origin. They were not so tolerant in all their notions as their children have become, and according to their sense of propriety and duty they maintained a strict watch over all things pertaining to the moral and spiritual welfare of the good people of the town. In these days of modern degeneracy, their inquisitorial proceedings would have excited no small degree of indignation, and their prying committees would have met with many a severe rebuff.

Soon after the settlement of Rev. Mr. Payson, a committee was chosen to see that all the inhabitants duly and constantly attended meeting on the Sabbath, and to report the names of those who were delinquent. The latter were inevitably fined.

A Mr. Abel Baldwin, who lived on the farm where Moses Hale now lives, once came within the number of the unfortunate delinquents. He was consequently fined. He made his appearance before Thomas Cowdin, Esqr., who was then living in what is now

---

*Before Fitchburg was set off, two or more school-houses had been built in the precincts of Lunenburg, and the people of what was afterwards Fitchburg paid their proportion of the tax for the support of schools. It would be injustice to many persons not to mention the exertions which they made in their individual capacity, for the education of their children. Many private or subscription schools were opened—some with very competent teachers. The children received *three-fourths* of their instruction in this way. This is quite a palliation for the conduct of the town in its corporate capacity.

called the Old City, and paid his fine; but he did so with evident reluctance, and an unwilling mind. He looked about him and seemed to think that the place, as well as the people, was entitled to a share of the blame, for so rigid a restriction upon his liberty. He expressed his opinion that the place would not prosper, and that a curse would follow it. He accordingly gave to it the name of *Sodom*—and it is called Sodom unto this day.[*]

At this period of our history, when there was a paucity of subjects to engage public attention, many trivial circumstances, which now would excite no interest beyond the sphere of the individuals immediately interested, gradually worked themselves into affairs of public importance, and came under the cognizance of the town. The minister, the meeting-house, the pews, and even the petty differences between man and man, frequently presented questions which were decided by the town.

To show the views and understanding of the people then, their disposition to assume a general interest and oversight over each other's affairs, I will mention several circumstances, as they appear on the town Records.

Phinehas Steward and Edward Scott respectively laid claim to a certain pew in the meeting-house. This important affair coming before the town, it was "Voted and agreed upon by the two parties on account of the Pew in contest, and by Phinehas Steward, which Pew Edward Scott claims is given up by said Steward to said Scott, upon condition that said Scott pays 30 shillings, and pays also what money the Town's committee dignified the Pew ground at to said Steward,—and furthermore, both parties, that is, said Edward Scott and said Phinehas Steward, each of them agreed and actually signed the Town's vote, both of them never to make any more uneasiness further about said Pew, if

---

[*]He was a carpenter and joiner by trade, and withal a very respectable man. Being a Baptist— a *rara avis* in those days—he did not choose to unite in the worship of those of a different persuasion. The town wickedly persecuted him for conscience' sake.

the money be paid by said Scott in one week from this day, being the 23d day of May, 1768.

(*Signed*) EDWARD SCOTT.
PHINEHAS STEWARD.

Attest, THOS. COWDIN, *Town Clerk.*

It appears that one Eliphalet Mace, then living where Jacob H. Merriam now lives, in giving in his invoice to the assessors, was actuated by a disposition which has not become entirely obsolete in the town at the present day. He quietly kept back some few articles of his property—not wishing to appear too vainglorious about his worldly possessions. The town took cognizance of the matter, and soon came to the conclusion that, though the said Mace might be poor in spirit, he was not so very poor in earthly goods. They accordingly voted that he should be fined forty shillings for giving in a false invoice. Some time afterward, the anger of the town was considerably abated, and the fine of Mace was abated in proportion. It was voted that twenty-eight shillings of it be deducted—so the unfortunate man was fined only twelve shillings for his untimely modesty.

In a few years after the incorporation of the town, several roads were opened, and a considerable sum was expended upon bridges. The road from South Fitchburg (leading over the arched bridge, and so by the dwelling-house of Alonzo P. Goodridge, to the Old City) was opened in 1765. The road from Pearl Hill by the dwelling-houses of Isaiah Putnam and Amos Wheeler, till it comes into the old road to Lunenburg, was accepted in 1766. It is worthy of remark that in these, and in many other instances, the land which was needed for the roads, was given by the owners thereof. They asked for no jury to decide upon the amount of damage which they sustained by these improvements. In the spring of 1770, the town found it necessary to rebuild the bridges carried away by the " late freshet." But they did not rebuild them sufficiently high from the water, for in 1771, the records say that it voted " to rebuild the bridges carried away and *damnified* by the floods." The town also very magnanimously "voted to pay for the *rum* expended at the bridges."

The good people of Fitchburg being vexed by the intrusion of "cattel" belonging to persons having no "interest" in the town, they promptly forbade the entrance of all such "cattel," and proceeded to build a "pound with logs." It was enjoined " that every person in town come and work at said pound, or pay his proportion." It was a common practice for them, however, to vote that their own "Hoaggs Go at Large lawfuly Yokt and Ringd,"—as the erudite Town Clerk has recorded it.

It is well known that, at this period, the disputes and difficulties between Great Britain and her Colonies were fast approaching a crisis. Soon after the French power in Canada had been crushed in 1759, the British Ministry began to turn their thoughts towards raising a revenue in America. Their first step in this proceeding was to direct the collector for the port of Boston to apply to the civil authority for "*Writs of Assistance*," to command the aid of all sheriffs and constables in breaking open houses, stores, ships, and packages of all sorts, to search for articles prohibited by the "*Acts of Trade*,"—a series of acts which had been passed to favor the West India merchants, and which had nearly annihilated the commerce of the Colonies. These acts had been mostly evaded by non-importation and smuggling.

The legality of the "Writs" was doubted, and the question came before the Superior Court, for decision, in February, 1761. By the powerful assistance of James Otis, the Writs were defeated. His masterly speech on this occasion first awakened the Colonists to the real danger of the threatened course of the ministry. They saw, in the pretended right of Parliament of taxing them to an unlimited extent, the germ of tyranny which would destroy their liberties; and they wisely resolved to destroy the monster in its shell, before it should acquire sufficient strength to crush them in its folds. They knew that their charter gave them the right to tax themselves, and that every exercise of this right on the part of the parliament was an infringement upon their chartered privileges. They were not actuated by the sordid love of money, but by the nobler love of liberty. They had freely poured forth their treasure and their blood in the preceding wars, and now they claimed the privilege of taxing themselves. They contended that "Taxation and Representation were inseparable;" while Parliament claimed the right to "bind the Colonies in all cases whatever." This was the point on which the dispute turned.

In the years 1763, 4 and 5, the commerce of the Colonies was nearly at a stand, in consequence of the " Sugar Act," and the " Stamp Act." Their operation was defeated by non-importation and smuggling. To the great joy of the Colonists, the Stamp Act was repealed in 1766, and the importation of goods was greater than ever. A cloud was soon thrown over the prosperity which everywhere began to be visible. The " Revenue Act " was passed in 1768. Again the people of Massachusetts took the lead in asserting the liberties of the Colonies, and they acted promptly and effectually.

By means of associations, speeches, circulars and pamphlets, the rights of the Colonies, and the dangers with which they were threatened, were fully discussed and laid before the people.

In September, 1768, the Selectmen of Fitchburg received a letter from the Selectmen of Boston, requesting them to call a town-meeting, and then to take into consideration the critical condition of government affairs, and to choose an agent to come to Boston to express there the views, wishes, and determination of the people of Fitchburg on this important subject. A town meeting was accordingly called, and this town, in conjunction with Lunenburg, chose Hon. Edward Hartwell, of the former place, to be their agent. What his instructions were, the records do not state; but their subsequent proceedings leave no doubt but that thus early the people were resolved upon maintaining their rights.

J

The firm resistance with which the projects of the British government were received, served to strengthen the determination of the Ministry to carry their point, at all hazards. Troops were stationed in Boston to overawe the inhabitants. Acts of increased severity were passed. The colonists saw that they must yield or maintain their rights at the point of the bayonet. They did hesitate between the alternatives. They did not prepare for the encounter under the impulse of the moment, but calmly deliberated upon the propriety of every measure. The pens of Otis, Adams, and their associates, were ever busy. The acts of the government were severely scrutinized, and the rights of the Colonies most ably vindicated and maintained. But one sentiment pervaded the community, and that was a fixed determination to preserve inviolate their freedom.

The people of Boston took the lead in these measures of resistance, and were nobly seconded by the inhabitants of the other towns. They sought an expression of opinion from every town on the all-engrossing subject of dispute, in order that they might know what they could rely upon, if it should be necessary to meet the obstinacy of Great Britain with open rebellion.

In November, 1773, another letter was received from the town of Boston, requesting the inhabitants of Fitchburg to pass such resolves concerning their rights and privileges as free members of society, as they were willing to die in maintaining—and to send them, in the form of a report, to the Committee of Correspondence in Boston. The town was not unmindful of this invitation. A meeting was held on the first day of December following. A copy of the records of this meeting will convey a good idea of the views and feelings of the inhabitants on these important subjects. The record is as follows:—

"At a Legal town meeting in Fitchburg on the first day of December, 1773, in order to take into consideration the letters of correspondency from the town of Boston—the Town made choice of Mr. Isaac Gibson as moderator for the government of said meeting. These said letters were read before the town—and after the town had deliberated thereon with zeal and candor, unanimously agreed to choose a committee of seven men, and chose Mr. Isaac Gibson, Capt. Reuben Gibson, Messrs. Phinehas Hartwell, Ebenezer Wood, Ebenezer Bridge, Kendall Boutelle, and Solomon Steward, as a committee to consider of our constitutional rights and privileges in common with other towns in this Province, together with the many flagrant infringements that have been made thereon, and to report at the adjournment;—and then this meeting was adjourned to the 15th of the same month. At the adjourned meeting the committee reported as follows:—

"Having with great satisfaction perused the circular letters from the committee of correspondency for the Town of Boston, wherein are so clearly held forth our rights and privileges as Englishmen and Christians, and also a list of the many infringements that have been made thereon, which letters of correspondence we highly approve of and unanimously consent unto, and resolve to stand fast in the liberty and rights wherewith our Gracious Sovereign Kings have made us free by an undeniable Charter and Decree from them, their heirs and successors forever;—And we are fully persuaded that liberty is a most precious gift of God our Creator to all mankind, and is of such a nature that no person or community can justly part with it, and consequently that no men, or number of men, can have a right to exercise despotism or tyranny over their fellow creatures;—and, to save us from such extreme wretchedness, we believe the vigilance and combined endeavors of this people are necessary—and we hope through the favor of Divine Providence, will be effectual. And we think it our indispensable duty as men, as Englishmen and Christians, to make the most public declaration in our power on the side of liberty. We have indeed an ambition to be known to the world and to posterity as friends of liberty—and we desire to use all proper means in our contracted sphere to promote it, and we are necessitated to view the enemies of liberty as enemies of our lawful sovereign, King

George, and his illustrious family;—because tyranny and slavery
are fundamentally repugnant to the British Constitution. But in
declaring our present thoughts and resolutions, we are moved by
a principle of humanity and benevolence to the people of Great
Britain, whose happiness is so involved with ours that the oppressors
and depredations endued on us by tyrannical government, must be
essentially detrimental to them. We therefore earnestly supplicate
the Deity to preserve them from political lethargy, and so from
the most shameful and· miserable bondage. And we are fond
of having our little obscure names associated with our American brethren as instruments in the hands of God, to save Britain
from that complete destruction which is now meditating and visibly
impending. We wish, therefore, our countrymen to join with us
in praying for a spirit of reformation on the inhabitants both
of England and America, because righteousness is the exalta-
tion and glory of any society. And we humbly hope that being
so late in giving our sentiments upon affairs so deeply interesting to the American Colonies in general, and to this Province in particular, will not be imputed to our being unaffected
with the alarming and unconstitutional encroachments that have
been made upon our civil rights and privileges,—for we assure
you we will not be wanting at all times according to our small
ability, in procuring and promoting all lawful and constitutional
measures proper for the continuance of all our rights and privileges, both civil and religious. And we think it our duty on
this occasion, in behalf of ourselves and our dear country, to
express our unfeigned gratitude to the respectable Gentlemen
of the Town of Boston, for the light and counsel that they
have presented to us in their circular letters, and their many
generous efforts in the defence of our privileges, and in the
cause of liberty,—and in our earnest prayers to Almighty God,
that they may be animated still to proceed and prosper in such a
noble and generous design, and finally may they receive that
most ample and durable reward;—And that these resolves be

recorded in our town book of records, and that the town Clerk give an attested copy to the said committee, to be communicated to the committee of correspondence for the town of Boston. And with respect to the East Tea—forasmuch as we are now informed that the town of Boston and the neighboring towns have made such noble opposition to said Tea's being brought into Boston, subject to a duty so directly tending to the enslaving of America—it is our opinion that your opposition is just and equitable; and the people of this town are ready to afford all the assistance in their power to keep off all such infringements. THOMAS COWDIN, *Town Clerk.*"

We learn from the above what the sentiments of the people of this town were concerning the course which Great Britain was pursuing towards her colonies. They believed that it was oppressive and unjust, and that they, as freemen, ought by no means to submit to it. Though living far back in the interior, they heartily responded to the noble and patriotic sentiments which animated the bosoms of the people of Boston, and acquired for their favorite place of meeting (Faneuil Hall) that most beautiful of names—the " Cradle of Liberty."

We see also that with respect to the tax on tea, the opinions of the people of this town accorded with those of the inhabitants of Boston. They were not only willing to forego that luxury, but even to take up arms against it, rather than submit in the least to an arbitrary mode of taxation. They offered support and assistance in an hour when none but the most faithful remained firm. They were determined and courageous, but with their courage was mingled discretion. That their zeal had no kindred with outrage is shown in the following instructions which they gave to their representative, in May, 1774. This representative, Dr. John Taylor, of Lunenburg, was chosen jointly by the towns of Lunenburg and Fitchburg, and a committee consisting of Isaac Gibson and Phinehas Hartwell, of this town, and three gentlemen of Lunenburg, was directed to draft instructions by which he should be governed in the House of Representatives. They were as follows :—

" Dr. John Taylor—*Sir :* As you are chosen by the towns of Lunenburg and Fitchburg to represent them in the Great and General Court for the present year, we think it our duty, under the present alarming circumstances of public affairs, to give you the following instructions, viz :—That you bear testimony against all riotous practices, and all other unconstitutional proceedings, and that you do not, by any means whatsoever, either directly or indirectly give up any of our charter rights and privileges, and that you use your endeavors that those that we have been abridged of, may be restored to us, and that you use your influence that provision be made for the discountenancing all unwarrantable practices with respect to bribery in those that set themselves up as candidates for representatives for the people, either by the way of treats or entertainments, which may have been too frequent a practice in many places,—and further, we would have you move in the General Assembly that there might be a Congress and union with all the Provinces, and in case anything extraordinary should happen or appear, that you should immediately notify your constituents. There are many things of lesser importance that we must leave discretionary with yourself, trusting that you will often revolve in your mind how great a trust is devolved upon you, and that you will give constant attendance, so far as you are able, to the business to which you are appointed ;—and we hope that you will be actuated by a spirit of impartiality, free from private views and sinister ends."

Whether Dr. John Taylor moved in the General Assembly for the Congress, in accordance with his instructions, I do not know, but the deputies of such a congress met in Philadelphia in September, 1774.

A Provincial Congress, of which John Hancock was the president, met at Concord, on the second Tuesday of October, and after adjourning to Cambridge, drew up a plan for the immediate defence of the Province. They resolved that at least one-fourth part of the Militia should be enrolled as minute-men, i. e. should be prepared to march at a minute's warning, on any emergency. To the Congress which took this decisive step, this town sent Capt. David Goodridge, as delegate. The members were supported and paid for their services by *contribution;* and this town voted that if there should be any overplus, after paying their delegate, it should be appropriated to the purchase of *powder*—the people seeming to be well convinced that something more noisy than talk would be expended before the dispute should be finished.

At this time, (October) the Selectmen paid 14*l.* 4*s.* ($47.33) for powder, lead, and flints; and in November, in accordance with the vote of Congress, forty men were enlisted to form a company of minute-men. The town also voted to indemnify the constables for refusing to pay over the money which had been assessed by the Province, into the hands of Harrison Gray, Esq. It was also voted to indemnify the assessors for refusing to return the names of such constables, though requested. These were certainly very bold measures, and well calculated to bring on the tug of war.

On the 10th day of January, 1775, the town chose Capt. David Goodridge a delegate to the Provincial Congress which was to meet at Cambridge on the first day of February. A committee was also chosen to review and inspect the "Minute-Company," as it was called—and Joseph Fox was appointed to receive any article which the inhabitants of the town might see fit to contribute to the relief of the poor of Boston, who were now suffering under the vengeance of the British Parliament, for the *tea* affair, &c.

It will be thus seen that the town was prepared for the important crisis which was now at hand — the opening scene of the Revolution. A small detachment of troops had been sent from Boston in February, to destroy the military stores collected at Salem, and those at Concord were exposed to the same danger.

The 19th of April, the day on which the troops of Great Britain and her Colonies first came in hostile collision, had now dawned. The British troops reached Concord at seven o'clock, A. M., and the "Alarm" was fired in Fitchburg at 9 o'clock in front of the store of Dea. Ephraim Kimball, which then stood on the site of the present Stone Mill, in the Old City. This was the appointed rendezvous of the "Minute-men," where their guns and equipments were kept, ready for instant action. This company had spent the previous day at drill. They assembled here as soon as possible, when the alarm was given, and, being joined by several volunteers, about fifty men took up the line of march for Concord, under the command of Capt. (afterwards Col.) Ebenezer Bridge. They arrived at their destination in the course of the same evening, but in sufficient season only to witness some of the effects of the action, viz: some dead bodies, and several wounded British soldiers, whom their brethren, in the rapidity of their flight, had left to the mercy of the people. The remains of the British detachment were, by this time, safely entrenched on Bunker Hill.

The anxiety which prevailed throughout the town, on this day, may be imagined. Exaggerated reports of the force and intentions of the enemy were spread, and every thing was veiled in uncertainty. A large proportion of the able bodied men had marched forward at a moment's warning to encounter dangers, how great no one could tell. Many a one, in bidding farewell to a father, husband or brother, felt that the separation might be eternal.

Those who remained were not inattentive to the physical wants of the departed. A large baggage wagon well filled with provisions was immediately sent forward, under the care of Thomas Cowdin, Jr.

It thus appears that when the time of action came, the people of the town did not fail to make their deeds correspond with their professions.

As there was no immediate need for their services, a large number of the men soon returned home. The provisions which they did not consume, were afterwards sold, and the proceeds, amounting to $48.50, were given, by a vote of the town, to their minister, Rev. John Payson—on the principle, perhaps, that if the money was not wanted by those who fought our battles, it could not be better appropriated than by being given to one who earn-estly prayed for our success.

The army, which was now assembled around Boston, was com-posed of "Minute-men" and others, who had rushed to the scene of action upon the first alarm of the battle of Lexington. It was necessary to proceed to organize this body of men immedi-ately. Measures to this effect were taken, and the men were regularly enlisted, formed into companies and regiments. A com-pany was enlisted (most of them for eighteen months) and organ-ized from among the volunteers of Lunenburg and Fitchburg. Of this company, John Fuller, of Lunenburg, was captain, Eben-ezer Bridge, of Fitchburg, lieutenant, and Jared Smith, of Lu-nenburg, ensign.

After this period, several of the inhabitants joined the army at different periods, and for different lengths of time. As near as I can learn, about thirty were constantly in the army till the British troops evacuated Boston, in March, 1776.

It is not certainly known how many of the inhabitants of this town were engaged in the battle of Bunker Hill, but the num-ber was not far from ten or twelve. I have been able to get the names of four or five. John Gibson, a son of Isaac Gibson, (whose name has frequently occurred in the course of this history) was one of these. It is supposed that he was killed there, for he has never been seen or heard of since that day. He was last seen in the entrenchments, in the hottest of the fight,

K

bravely opposing the enemy with the breech of his gun. There cannot be much doubt but that he was finally overpowered and killed, though his body could not be recognized among the slain.

It may be worthy of remark that after this period, no soldier belonging to this town was killed during the continuance of the war, and that one only was severely wounded, some years after this.

On the 22d day of May, Joseph Fox was chosen a delegate to attend the Provincial Congress which assembled at the meeting house in Watertown, on the 31st of the same month. At the same town-meeting, it was voted to purchase forty bayonets, (which cost $26.) These were probably for the use of the standing company which had been formed several years previous, and of which Ebenezer Woods was commanding officer. How these bayonets were made to fit guns of different calibres, tradition has not informed us.

The warrant for a town-meeting in July deserves more particular notice, as differing from all previous and several subsequent ones. They had ever commenced in this form—" In his Majesty's name, you are hereby required to warn," &c. But this runs in the following manner: " In his Majesty's name, and in observance to the Provincial and Continental Congress' Resolves, you are required," &c. This course was probably dictated by that sound discretion which suggests the propriety of treating all authorities with due respect, they not knowing into whose hands they might fall. The town voted not to send a delegate to the Provincial Congress at Watertown, " by virtue of *that* warrant." Several of the succeeding warrants ran in the old form. In March, 1776, the town, by order of the General Court, chose a committee of correspondence, consisting of Reuben Gibson, Kendall Boutelle, Asa Perry, John Putnam and Silas Snow. This was the last occasion on which the people of Fitchburg acknowledged the authority of " his Majesty's name."

The warrant for a meeting in May ran thus: " In observance of the Colony Writ to us directed,—These are, in the name of the Government and People of the Massachusetts Bay, to will and require you," &c. At this meeting, it was voted *not* to send a representative to the General Court at Watertown.

The next town-meeting, which was held on the first day of July, 1776, shows what was the disposition of the inhabitants, when the important question of National Independence was submitted to them. The General Court then in session, had assured the Continental Congress that if they, in their wisdom, should deem it expedient to declare the Colonies free and independent, the people of this Colony would undoubtedly support them in the measure. The State Legislature, however, to make the thing certain, passed a resolve that each town should act individually on the important question. By virtue of this resolve, this town assembled on the first day of July. The proceedings of this meeting are as follows:—

" *Voted*, That if the Honorable Continental Congress should, for the safety of these United Colonies, declare them independent of the Kingdom of Great Britain, that we, the inhabitants of the 'town of Fitchburg, will, with our lives and fortunes, support them in the measure." This took place only three days previous to the adoption of the Declaration by Congress. The question was introduced there on Friday, the 7th of June, and was discussed on that day, on Saturday, and on the following Monday. Further debate was postponed till July 1st. It was during this interval that the question was submitted to the several towns of this Province. On the very day on which the question was resumed in Congress, the people of Fitchburg declared themselves ready to peril their lives and fortunes in the cause of freedom.

The declaration having been adopted, copies were sent by order of the Council, to the several towns of the State, where they were read from the pulpit, and then copied into the town Book of Records—there to remain as a perpetual memorial thereof."

In October, the question was submitted to this town, whether
they were willing that the then Representative House, together
with the Council, should make a form of government for the
State of the Massachusetts Bay. The town expressed their unwil-
lingness to this course, and drew up their reasons in the form
of a report, which was transmitted to the Legislature. It is as
follows: "As we are sensible that our situation demands a particular attention and due consideration in matters of the greatest
importance on so interesting concern for the public good, and
for the good order and benefit of the community and peace of
this State, — that as the end of government is the happiness
of the people, so the sole right and power of forming and establishing a plan thereof is essentially in the people. We are therefore unwilling that the present House of Representatives, together
with the Council, should make a form of government for this State.

Firstly—Because the present House were never elected by the
people to establish a form of government for this State, but for
ordering and governing the prudential affairs of this embarrassed
State, as necessity calls for their strict attention thereto.

Secondly—Because a large number of our worthy inhabitants
of this State is now engaged in the service of the United States
in opposing our unnatural enemies, who, we apprehend, ought, of
right, to have an equal voice in establishing a form of government
for this State, as those that are not engaged in the army. But
provided the present House of Representatives, together with the
Council, should proceed to make a form of government, *Resolved*,
That it is the opinion of this town that said form of government
should be made public for the perusal and inspection of the inhabitants, before the ratification thereof by the assembly."

It will be readily imagined that, under the severe pressure of
a harassing war, when all resources were heavily drawn upon to
furnish arms, ammunition, clothes and provisions for the army, to
supply funds for the payment of the soldiers, and to meet other
expenses incident to the state of public affairs, money, among the

inhabitants was not only exceedingly scarce, but that, in consequence of the successive draughts for soldiers, laborers were in
great demand, and their services commanded exorbitant prices.
The result of this was that the prices of all commodities and articles of consumption rose in proportion. The embarrassed condition
of our trade, previous to the commencement of the war, had also
tended to increase the scarcity of money; so that this anomaly
now presented itself—everything was exceedingly dear, and no one
had money to buy with. The General Court felt the evil, and
endeavored ineffectually to apply a remedy. They passed an act
for dividing the Commonwealth into districts, and ordering that a
committee should be chosen in each district, to fix upon certain
prices for labor and provisions,—which prices, when thus established, it should be unlawful for any one to exceed. This scheme
continued in operation for a few weeks, when it fell to the ground,
by common consent. It was found to operate unequally, and the
people would not submit to it.

Groton, Shirley, Townsend, Lunenburg and Fitchburg composed
one district. I have thought it might prove interesting to mention the prices which were affixed to some of the most important
articles, by the committee of these towns.

Labor of men, in summer, per day, -	50	cents.
" " winter, " " -	25	"
A carpenter, or housewright, per day, -	50	"
Wheat, per bushel, - -	$1.11	
Rye, " " - - -	73	"
Corn, " " - -	56	"
Oats, " " - - -	33	"
Pork, " pound, - -	6	"
Butter, " " - - -	12½	"
Beef, " " - -	6	"
Potatoes, per bushel, - -	17	"
Good sheep's wool, per lb., -	33	"
Men's stockings, of the best quality, -	1.00	

Men's shoes,	-	-	1.33
Lamb, mutton and veal, per lb.,		-	4½ cents.
Hay, per ton,	-	-	10.00
Pine boards, per thousand,	-	-	3.67
Clapboards, " "	-	-	10.67
Wheat flour, per 100 lbs.,	-	-	3.67
For a dinner, boiled and roasted,	-	17	"
For a dinner with only one of these,	-	14	"
For a mug of West India flip,	-	15½	"
For a mug of N. E. flip,	-	-	12½ "
Good cider, per barrel,	-	-	1.83
Men tailors, per day,	-	-	42 "
Women tailors, per day,	-	-	15½ "
Yard-wide cotton cloth,	-	-	58 "
House maids, per week,	-	-	42 "
Horse for one person to ride, per mile,		3⅛	"

There are indications that at this period (1777) the town began to grow weary of its burdens. There was no prospect of an immediate termination of the war—no prospect of "better times." The inhabitants were dilatory in furnishing their quotas of continental soldiers. The great bounty required for enlistments seemed too enormous to be offered. Those who felt disposed to go forth to the field of battle, looked upon their families, and saw that they must be left to poverty and want, unless they could depend upon the bounties for support. Of specie, but little was in the country, and paper money was rapidly depreciating in value. The resources of the country seemed to be nearly exhausted. It is not surprising, therefore, that the stoutest heart, at times, yielded to despondency. Yet there is one thing truly surprising. Amid all this gloom, when all were disheartened at the prospect before them, there were no general murmurs heard, as of old among the children of Israel, sighing for the "flesh-pots of Egypt"—no vain regrets that they had departed from under the protection of the British crown. On the contrary, the utmost vigilance was exercised to spy out, and hold up to public scorn the man who dared to show the least symptom of disaffection towards the American cause.

It was during this year that Phinehas Hartwell, whom, in the language of the records, the town presumed to be firmly attached to the American cause, was appointed a committee to procure and lay before a special Court of Sessions of the Peace, " the evidence that may be had of the inimical disposition towards this or any of the United States, of any inhabitant of this town, who shall be charged by the freeholders, and other inhabitants of said town." Indeed, not only was enmity to the cause severely punished, but persons exhibiting luke-warmness were watched with a suspicious eye. Every one had to come up to the mark prescribed by public opinion, or expose himself to the effects of popular indignation. More than one inhabitant of this town was threatened with a coat of tar and feathers, and even with the destruction of his house. Such persons had to walk very circumspectly to shelter themselves from ebulitions of popular feeling. They were even compelled to mount the head of a barrel, and in this conspicuous, though humbling condition, promise to the assembled majesty of the town, a greater love for the American cause, and a more strict obedience to the will of the people. Among this unfortunate class was our old friend, Thomas Cowdin, who, though in other respects a very popular man, and a very noted inn-keeper, was shorn of all his municipal honors in 1775, and was not again admitted to the confidence of the town till towards the close of the war. This summary process induced those who entertained inimical dispositions, to keep their opinions to themselves.

Though the burthen of the war was now pressing heavily upon a town which was not highly favored in the possession of worldly goods, the people did not despair of the cause of Independence. They continued to labor steadily to the utmost of their ability, and this year (1777) voted to raise $288 for purchas-

ing guns and ammunition for the town's use. In compliance with
an act of the General Court, they chose a committee, who had
full power and authority to supply with the necessaries of life, at
the town's expense, all those families of the soldiers who were engaged in the Continental service.

The wretched state of the currency at this time, was rendered
still worse by the improvident attempts of the Legislature to
remedy it. The General Court passed an act for putting large
sums of the bills of credit emitted by this State, on interest,
and sinking certain sums, less than ten pounds, in the possessors'
hands,—and prohibiting the circulation of the bills of any of the
United States, under a penalty of five pounds. The town was
opposed to this act, and sent to the General Court a remonstrance
to that effect.

In May, 1778, the town approved of the "articles of Confederation sent out by the Continental Congress." At this time the
new State Constitution was submitted to the people for their
approbation or disapprobation. The vote in this town was as
follows—For the Constitution, 22—against it, 4. The General
Court, at this period, called for four men for the Continental
army, and allowed the town $400 for this purpose. The town
treasurer was directed to give his note for the sum of $100 to
each soldier, or to borrow the money on the town's credit.

At the close of this year (1778) the period of the war of
the Revolution was half completed. It is impossible for us to
realize, at the present day, how completely that struggle called
into exercise every resource and the whole energy of every
individual throughout the community. How low soever might
be his condition, and however scanty might be his means of
supporting himself and his family, every man was called upon
to act—to do to the utmost of his ability, or rest under the
imputation of being a tory.

They who had money and the means of supplying the necessaries of an army, were compelled, not only by public opinion

but every legal power which an overwhelming majority could exert, to pour forth their wealth in aid of the common cause. They whom poverty marks as exempts, in ordinary cases, from any onerous services in their country's cause, could not now escape the all-searching requisition. The possession of physical strength was sufficient to call forth the poorest day laborer, though clothed in rags, and require of him the nerve of his right arm, to aid in the defence of his country.

The exertions made by the people of this town, in the early part of the war, while the enemy were in possession of Boston, have already been mentioned. Their entire military strength was put in requisition. Their enthusiasm was at its height, and the pay was good. After this period the necessity of adopting some regular system was felt. The General Court required the town to furnish a certain number of men whenever the State was called upon to make out a quota. These men were selected by a committee, and a bounty was paid to them, which was assessed by a general rate upon the town. In the latter years of the war, it was proposed by the Legislature, and adopted in this town, to divide the people into classes—each class consisting of about twelve or fourteen individuals, according to their wealth. The person first named in each class was entrusted with the keeping of its accounts, and the general management of its concerns. Whenever the town was called upon for soldiers, the classes were required to furnish a man in rotation—the burthen being equalized among them as nearly as possible. When called upon to furnish a man for three years or during the war, they were obliged to offer him, "over and above" what he would receive from the United States, as a soldier's pay, the sum of $300 as a bounty; and as the currency was fluctuating, and nearly worthless, the notes were made payable in produce, at a market value. When no one of a class was willing to volunteer on these conditions, it was usual to hire some other individual. When this could not be done, the members of the class were compelled to cast lots among themselves, to determine who of them should go; and he upon whom the unlucky lot fell, had to shoulder his musket and march, or find a substitute at some rate. This sometimes happened to one whose little property could scarcely survive the shock of taking from it the sum of one, two, or three hundred dollars to hire a substitute.

Notes were frequently given in these cases, which afterwards came before the town, with strong arguments and powerful appeals from those who were compelled to pay them, showing the manifest injustice that a single individual should be required to pay towards supporting the common cause so much more than his townsmen generally; and the town was accordingly asked to pay those notes by an assessment upon the inhabitants.

It was frequently voted to ascertain what each individual had done towards supporting the war, and to equalize the burthen; but unfortunately they could get no farther than this. The demands upon the town had been so frequent, and taxes of course so heavy, that generosity towards one another was not to be expected. The reports of committees chosen to investigate this subject, were laid before the town, and immediately voted down or not accepted. Each one, previous to an investigation, seemed to think that his sacrifices had exceeded those of his neighbor; but when a report had been made, and it appeared that a majority would be called upon to pay, instead of receiving something, the fate of such a report is not surprising.

The average number of men which the town kept in the field from this period till the close of the war, is not accurately known —but it was not far from fifteen or twenty. This must have brought upon the several classes an expense of at least $4000.

If the records be examined to ascertain what sums the town paid, in its corporate capacity, towards defraying the expenses of the war during the last five years of its continuance, the subject will be attended with considerable difficulty. The currency, in which the taxes were assessed, varied monthly. But from certain known data, an approach may be made towards the actual sum. During these five years, there were paid for fourteen hundred pounds of beef, for clothing for the army, and for the hire of soldiers, whom the town in its corporate capacity employed, about $7250. This sum was assessed upon the whole town, in addition to large sums which the several classes were obliged to pay for soldiers, hired by them respectively.

Let it be remembered also, that at this time, when all kinds of business had been brought nearly to a stand by the operation of the war,—when specie was almost unknown throughout the country, and the paper currency was but little better than so much brown paper, the ordinary expenses of the town—such as the support of the minister, of schools, of the highways and bridges, &c. &c., bore with extreme rigor upon the inhabitants.

At the commencement of the war, gold and silver were scarce articles; and it was soon found that if something could not be devised as a substitute for the precious metals, the patriots must give up the contest, and surrender all hope of gaining Independence. Congress ordered the issuing of notes, or bills to a large amount, promising to redeem them at a convenient season. This currency, called Continental Money, soon came into extensive circulation. The bills, instead of being executed in the masterly style of our bank note engravings, were rude, coarse prints, on coarser paper, and consequently were easily counterfeited. The British, actuated by the double motive of making money and ruining the credit of our government, flooded the country with counterfeits so well executed that they could not be distinguished from the true ones. In 1777, the bills began to depreciate; and all intelligent men soon saw that it would be impossible for the government ever to fulfil their pledge of redeeming them. The government, not being able, or not choosing to devise any other means to raise the credit of the bills, in an evil hour made them a legal tender for the payment of all debts due.

The consequences of this measure may be seen at a glance.

Never, since the time of the flood, were debtors more ready and anxious to pay their debts, or creditors more unwilling to receive their money. Of money, such as it was, there was no scarcity, and miserably poor was he who could not count his thousands. Then was the sun of prosperity darkened upon the prospects of those upon whom it is usually supposed to shine with peculiar favor. I refer to the lenders of money. Hundreds who before were in comfortable, if not affluent circumstances—more than supported by the income of their money — experienced the singular satisfaction of having every debt paid them, and, while gazing upon their masses of money, reflecting that they were reduced to poverty.

Elias Haskell, who has already been mentioned as once having owned all the land on which our pleasant village now stands, beside other tracts in the town, was one who by this measure was reduced from affluence to poverty.

If this sacrifice of so many men's property was made for the American cause, ought not the sufferers to have been indemnified by our government? Many a soldier who, instead of sacrificing any property, received adequate pay for his services, has been favored with a pension ; but who has been heard to lift up a voice in pleading the cause of those who sacrificed their thousands ?

It may be interesting at this time to give a slight sketch of the rate of the depreciation of this currency. On the first of January, 1777, it was at par. First of January 1778, $1.00, *specie*, was worth $4.50 *Continental ;* first of January 1779, $1.00 *specie* was worth $8.38 *Continental ;* first of January 1780, $1.00 *specie* was worth $32.50 *Continental.* At a town meeting in February, 1780, it was voted that the inhabitants should be allowed *three dollars* per hour for their labor on the highways. At the same meeting it was voted to raise the sum of $8000, to assist in supporting the families of continental soldiers. In July, it was voted to raise $166,666.00 to hire soldiers with. In the October following, a committee of the town contracted for 4800 pounds of beef, and agreed to pay $26,000 for it, or at a rate of more than

$5.00 per pound. In March, 1781, Phinehas Sawyer and John Carter were chosen collectors of taxes; and, refusing to serve in that capacity, they were severally fined by the town in the sum of $900—which was considered equal to $10, the usual fine in such cases. At the same meeting the town appropriated the sum of $20,000 for the repair of highways, and allowed each person $5 per hour for his labor.

Rev. John Payson, then minister of the town, who was settled on the original sum of 60l., came very near being starved, though the poor man could not complain that his salary was not paid very promptly. Yet he was not suffered to come to absolute want, for in March, 1778, the town chose a committee to carry a subscription paper among the inhabitants, that they might contribute " the necessaries of life or anything they pleased," for his support. The committee reported that Mr. Payson expressed himself as " well satisfied with what the town had done." In October of the same year, he received $1000, and in November, $266 more, (equivalent, in all, to nearly $184) as his salary. In 1780, the town voted to pay him $11,000, to make up the depreciation which had already occurred. Every one will see that with a currency so fluctuating as this, all business must come to a stand, unless another " circulating medium" be devised. And such was the case. Notes were generally given to pay to the bearer so many bushels of corn, or rye. Sometimes they promised to pay in " hard money." When in 1781, " nine continental men" were called for, the town voted to pay them each $100 in " hard money," and an agent was despatched to Boston, to borrow the same, on the town's credit. This year the town paid John Thurston 106 bushels of corn " for the services of his son Stephen in the Continental army."

In May, 1779, the town voted unanimously (casting 45 votes) in favor of a new State Constitution. In August, Capt. Thomas Cowdin was chosen a delegate to attend a Convention which was to meet at Cambridge on the first of September, for the purpose of forming a new State Constitution. At the same time, Dr. Thaddeus McCarty was appointed a delegate to a Convention at Worcester, for the purpose of regulating the prices of commodities and articles in general use. The town voted to abide by the prices established by this convention, but in a short time individuals saw fit to fix their own prices to their articles, and the labor of the convention fell to the ground.

In May, 1780, the present Constitution of the State was submitted to the people, for their consideration. The inhabitants of Fitchburg voted unanimously (65 votes) in favor of adopting it.

In September, votes were given for Governor. John Hancock received sixty-three votes, and James Bowdoin one.

In October, Capt. Thomas Cowdin was chosen to represent the town in the first General Court under the new Constitution.

In 1781 and '2, Rev. Mr. Payson received 100*l*., in "hard money," as his salary, but subsequently it was reduced to the former sum of 66*l*. 13*s*. 8*d*.

In September, 1782, David McIntire was chosen a delegate to the Convention at Worcester, assembled "to take into consideration the grievances Worcester County labored under"—and in March, 1784, he was appointed to attend a Convention at the same place, called by request of the town of Sutton.

In January, 1784, the town appropriated the sum of 474*l*. 13*s*. 4*d*.,—"the first moiety of the Continental tax granted by the General Court May, 1782," and in May it was voted to raise 80*l*. "to discharge an execution in the hands of the high sheriff against the town, *for deficiency of beef*."

I have already spoken of the difficulty of our attaining, at the present day, to an exact computation of the expenses, and forming a correct idea of the exertions which the war of the Revolution caused to the people of this town. All calculations based on data derived from the town Records, can be only an approximation to the actual amount. From 1778 to 1783—the last five years of the war—a period in which there occurred many events of sufficient interest to call out the whole body of voters—I can find no town meeting at which there appeared to be more than seventy voters. The town contains now seven times that number. Let it be remembered that at that time, between the dwelling-house of Jonas Marshall and the Old City, there was not a single building. The whole of the village, where there is now so much wealth—where the inhabitants are clustered so thickly together—was then considered worth only a few dollars. If the wealth and resources of the town, at the present time be estimated as ten times greater than at that period, it will not be far from the truth. If then the amount which the people then contributed annually be multiplied by ten, would not the product form a tax which would be considered enormous—and this too when it was so difficult to meet the current expenses of the town, and when the expenses of the "*classes*," for hiring soldiers and procuring substitutes were so great?

To learn what the Revolutionary war cost this country, we must search minutely into the history of each town. We there may see what difficulties were encountered, and what generous sacrifices were made. To say that the people of this town bore themselves gallantly through the war, is not saying enough—though their exertions did not exceed those of their neighbors. They continued to exhibit a firmness, a devotedness to the cause they had espoused, which was every way worthy of our fathers. There were a few, indeed, who looked with an eye of coldness upon the attempt of the patriots. They feared that the Colonies, weak and unprovided as they were, would not be able to contend successfully with the gigantic power of Great Britain; or the sentiment of *loyalty* was so firmly fixed in their minds that they beheld with horror any attempts to subvert the authority of their King. Such were compelled to yield to the mighty current of public opinion, and contribute their share, however unwillingly, to promote the common cause.

But the troubles above enumerated, were not all which this

town had to contend with during the struggle for Independence.
The Small Pox,—that pestilential and terrible disease now happily disarmed of its terrors—was then considered one of the
most dreadful maladies that ever afflicted the human family.
This disease made its appearance here in 1776, and spread an
alarm far and near. Vaccination, or innoculation for the kine
pox, as a preventive for the small pox, was then unknown in
this country. The only means then known to prevent the rav-
ages of this fatal disease, was innoculation for the small pox.
The disease, even then, was sometimes fatal, and equally in-
fectious as when taken in the natural way. It was necessary,
therefore, that a place remote from the habitations of men
should be selected, where they who attempted to avert the
fatality of the small pox by innoculation for the same disease,
might repair during the period of sickness.

Dr. Thaddeus McCarty, a physician of this town, in connection with Dr. Israel Atherton, a distinguished physician of
Lancaster, established a hospital for this purpose, on Buck hill,
so called, in the rear of Philip F. Cowdin's dwelling house, in
the year 1776. To this place the people of this and the neighboring towns repaired, and had the small pox by innoculation.
Notwithstanding all precautions, several died here; and instead
of being carried to the grave-yards of their respective towns,
they were buried on the hill on which they died. This was
owing to a foolish notion then prevalent, that if these remains
should ever be disturbed, they would communicate the dreaded
disease to any one that might come in contact with them. Of
the large number of patients who were here, it is not known
that more than five died. If any should take the trouble to
visit the place, they may find in the skirts of the wood a
single grave, the headstone of which bears this inscription:—
"Josiah Fairbanks, of Lancaster, died March 12th, 1777."

Dr. McCarty, it appears, labored incessantly to alleviate the
pains of those who were suffering under this loathsome disorder,

and to allay the fears of those who were well. For his exertions in this praiseworthy cause, the good people of the town showed their gratitude by propagating a report that either he or his friends introduced the disease into the place for the purpose of giving him a good business.

Dr. Thaddeus McCarty was a son of Rev. Thaddeus McCarty, of Worcester, and came into this town in 1772 or '3. He was then a young man, and the first physician who resided in this place. He married a daughter of Capt. Thomas Cowdin, and lived in the house now occupied by one or more families of color, in the Old City. He was a man of good education, and reputed to have been skilful in his profession. So long as he remained in the town, he had great influence in public affairs. He removed from this town to Worcester in 1781. Remaining there a short time, he went to Keene, N. H., commenced business as a trader there, and in a few years died. His only child, a daughter, is the wife of John Stiles, a wealthy citizen of Worcester.

The first store opened in this town, was kept by Deacon Ephraim Kimball. This took place about the year 1772. The store was in a part of his dwelling house, which stood where the Stone Factory now stands. After trading here several years, he commenced purchasing real estate, and lived on several farms which he successively bought. In 1794, he, in connection with Jonas Marshall, (as has been mentioned in another place) built a dam and a saw-mill where the red, or Rollstone Factory now is. In 1797, he built the house where Daniel Tuttle now lives, and there he spent the remainder of his days.

Joseph Fox, Esq. came into this town from Littleton, in 1772, and occupied a part of the "Boutelle" house. He was a shoe-maker by trade, and plied himself to his calling for some little time in his dwelling house. He commenced trading by bringing goods in his saddle-bags from Boston, and retailing them from his shoemaker's bench. Soon after this he opened the red store which constituted one in the block of old buildings which stood between the main road and the Stone Factory. He was a man of great influence in the town, and died a few years since, after having acquired a large property.

About this time, William Hitchborn came from Boston, and built one of the houses in the block above mentioned. He was a hatter by trade, and a Justice of the Peace. In 1781, he was one of three persons licensed by the selectmen to sell tea. He appears not to have attracted much notice till it was understood that he was about to procure a commission in the Peace, which in those days was a most important circumstance. An urgent remonstrance, headed by Dea. David Goodridge, and signed by a large number of citizens, was sent to the Fountain of Honor, protesting earnestly against the appointment. But a brother of Hitchborn then living in Boston, was too powerful, and the esquireship was obtained, despite the remonstrance. Hitchborn soon became very poor, sold his establishment to Joseph Fox, and returned to Boston.

It thus appears that the "Old City," as it is now called, was the distinguished part of the town—having the meeting-house, the tavern, the stores, the doctor, the hatter, and the miller, all within its precincts.

David Gibson, son of Isaac Gibson of Pearl Hill, having learned the baker's trade, turned his eyes westward of the Old City, and in a daring moment, reckless of a rough soil and its rougher productions—such as pine stubs, hard-hack, grape-vines, &c. &c., built a bakery on the spot now occupied by the dwelling house of E. Torrey, Esq., and located his dwelling house directly opposite to it. This was the first house built in what is now called the Village—unless the house of Benjamin Danforth, which stood nearly where S. M. Dole's house now stands, preceded it.

Gibson went to Vermont in 1792, and Dr. Peter Snow, who succeeded Dr. McCarty in the practice of medicine in the town, moved into this house, and occupied it several years.

Not far from the time when Gibson's house was built, Benjamin Kemp built a house where Jonas Marshall's brick house now stands. But this was so far west that it was not then considered as forming a component part of the "middle of the town."

Joseph Fenno, lived in a log house a few steps beyond the brick-yard brook—and nearly in front of Josiah Sheldon's present dwelling house. He afterwards built and occupied a house where Dea. Abel Downe now lives.

Capt. William Brown built the present dwelling house of Capt. Z. Sheldon, in the year 1783 or '4. He owned the mills and clothier's works in the Old City. He occupied this as his dwelling house at first, and afterwards as a tavern.

The houses built by David Gibson, by Benjamin Danforth, and by Capt. William Brown, were the only ones properly in the limits of the Village when the first Parish Meeting-house was built, in the year 1796.

In August, 1784, Dea. Kendall Boutelle and Thomas Stearns attended as delegates from this town, a Convention at Westminster, holden for the purpose of dividing the County of Worcester, or for devising means for that purpose; and in the following May, Dr. Jonas Marshall, Capt. Thomas Cowdin and Elijah Garfield attended a Convention at Lunenburg, for the same purpose. This has been, for a long time, a favorite object with the people in this town, but their efforts have never been crowned with the least success. They will probably be doomed for a long time to live at the distance of twenty-five miles from a court house and Jail.

After the declaration of peace, in 1783, a general stagnation of all kinds of business, as is usual in such cases, ensued. The United Colonies were burdened with a debt of forty millions of dollars, without any means of paying it. Congress, under the Confederation, had power only to advise the several states to adopt certain measures to meet the wants of the times.

But the states, actuated by a spirit of commercial rivalry and jealousy, would agree upon no uniform system. So far then from any measures being adopted to pay the public debt, even the interest of it remained unpaid.

The whole body of the people became alarmed, and all confidence was destroyed. Certificates of public debt lost their credit, and many officers and soldiers of the late army, who were poor, were compelled to sell these certificates at excessive reductions. They had fondly hoped that if they could establish their independence, and a government of their own choosing, public and private prosperity would everywhere abound, and that things would go on delightfully. Bitter, now, was their disappointment. Of money, there was next to none. The introduction of the precious metals had been prevented by the war and its attendant evils, and the paper money in circulation was worth about two shillings on the pound. Creditors became alarmed, and used every means in their power to secure their debts. Business was at a stand— men "failed,"—and lawyers were overwhelmed with employment. Never was the labor of the profession in greater demand, and never were Courts of Justice filled with more business. Massachusetts, for the purpose of maintaining her credit, loaded the people with excessive taxes. It was impossible for them to meet the demands made upon them. They knew not the origin of the evils, but supposed that there was some defect in the laws—that there were either too many, or not enough. Petitions were poured in upon the Legislature from all quarters—but the Legislature, like all deliberative bodies, moved slow. The patience of the people was entirely exhausted in seeing their property seized on "executions" issuing from these authoritive Courts, and, as petitions, remonstrances, and mild measures had failed to work out a remedy for their grievances, they determined to put down "WORCESTER, SS., In the name of the Commonwealth of Massachusetts," &c., by force of arms. Thus much it has been necessary to premise, to account for the origin of "Shays' Insurrection."

A large majority of the people of this, as well as the neighboring towns, were "Shaysites." In extenuation, though not in justification of their conduct, it may be remarked that their straightforward method of thinking did not lead them to comprehend the actual state of public affairs, and the necessity of sacrificing present convenience to future good. After a war of eight years' duration to avoid the evils of excessive and illegal taxation, they could not see what they had gained, if they were now to be subjected to severer taxation than ever. Gov. Bowdoin did not possess the confidence of the people, but was looked upon, as I have been told, rather as a "Britainer."

They did not break out into open rebellion here, though they stood ready, and undoubtedly would have done so, had they been goaded much further by the acts of the government. Their valor was fortunately well tempered with discretion. They knew that taking up arms against government was treason, and they knew that treason was a "hanging matter." However, they put no restraint upon their tongues, and their language savored strongly of rebellion. Some, it must be confessed, "swore terribly;" and the taxes ordered by the General Court were not all collected.

In June, 1786, Robert Burnham, Daniel Putnam, Thomas Stearns, Elijah Willard, and Phinehas Hartwell, were chosen a committee to take into consideration the circumstances of the town, its burdens, and to petition to the General Court for a redress of grievances. At the same meeting Elijah Willard was appointed a delegate to a Convention of the people of the County of Worcester, to take into consideration the public affairs of the Commonwealth.

Open rebellion having broken out in several places, and threats and demonstrations of warlike movements beginning to appear in others, the State Authorities were compelled to take notice of them, and resolved to put them down by an armed force. They had under their control the militia of the Commonwealth, and on their side all those who preferred good order, and an observance of the Laws—though somewhat objectionable—to open rebellion and civil war. Companies of the military were stationed in the infected districts, with orders to seize upon suspected persons, that they might be confined, or take an oath of allegiance and fidelity to the Commonwealth.

The town voted that Mr. Willard should attend the Convention at Worcester, and that they would defend his property if he should be taken in person by government for his attendance— provided he behaved in an orderly and peaceable manner — otherwise they prudently resolved that he should take all the risks upon his own shoulders.

In January, 1787, the town voted to petition the Legislature to have the Courts of Common Pleas, and of the Session, suspended till the choice of a new Representative house in the following May—also, to petition the government to liberate Capt. Shattuck and others, (who had been apprehended and imprisoned by the state (authorities) on their promising to behave as peaceable and faithful subjects of the Commonwealth,*—also to petition the government that the people might have the privilege of the Writ of *Habeas Corpus*. Phinehas Hartwell, Elijah Willard, and Dea. Ephraim Kimball were appointed to draft the above-mentioned petitions.

Thomas Cowdin, Esq., who firmly adhered to the government, was appointed in this town to administer the oath of allegiance and fidelity to those suspected persons who were compelled unwillingly to appear before him. A large company of soldiers, commanded by Capt. Johnson, was sent up from Lancaster to examine into the soundness of loyalty here. They had their quarters at the house of Capt. Thomas Cowdin for a few days, and then were removed to where J. L. Haynes now lives. Their business was to sally out by night, and sieze upon persons who happened to be suspected of entertaining dangerous

---

*Capt. Shattuck was a distinguished Shaysite of Pepperell, and was apprehended for his treasonable designs. He was most shamefully abused, and his life was threatened by those into whose hands he had fallen. His condition consequently excited the sympathy of all those who were disaffected towards the government.

opinions, and bring them by force before Capt. Cowdin, where they were compelled to take the oath, or be carried to jail.

It will readily be imagined that the people of the town were exceedingly indignant at such a state of things, when the Writ of *Habeas Corpus* was suspended, and martial law enforced. On more than one occasion were the citizens and soldiers on the point of engaging in deadly strife, which was prevented only by the latter yielding the point to the former. Some were quite ready, even with the halter dangling before their eyes, to oppose force to force, when they were awakened at dead of night by patroles of armed soldiers, who, strong in the protection of government, sometimes were guilty of shameful excesses.

Joshua Pierce, (who lived where Alonzo P. Goodridge now does) a warm Shaysite, was seized and brought before Esquire Cowdin, and, proving contumacious about the oath, he was held "in durance vile" for several days. Harsh measures were threatened to reduce him to subjection, but the soldiers feared the people, whose demonstrations were not to be mistaken, and they let him go.

The Gibsons of Pearl Hill were threatened with a nocturnal visit from the military. The wrath of these stout yeomen, who prided themselves not a little on their courage and strength, was kindled at this intimation. They ("Reuben and Jake"— as I have been told) stationed themselves on the common, and dared the soldiers to lay hands on them. The latter declined the contest, or a "battle royal" would probably have ensued.

Dr. Jonas Marshall was eagerly sought for, but he eluded their search by secreting himself in the cellar of "Upton's Tavern." He was not further troubled with unwelcome visits, in consequence of threats which he made, of furnishing the entry to his house with a trap door, so that if the soldiers desired to search his house, they might commence operations by examining the cellar first.

During this winter, (1786-7) the military company was removed to Townsend. They gave the finishing touch to their impudence by pressing into their service, for conveyance, both men and horses, for which no recompense was offered. On this occasion, Asa Perry, who hated the soldiers most cordially, did them the favor of turning them several times into snow-drifts— all by accident, of course.

The force headed by Shays himself having been dispersed, the agitation on this subject principally subsided in the following year. John Hancock was chosen Governor, and a majority of the House of Representatives were disposed to regard with a more favorable eye the interests of " the people." A check was placed upon the system of *sueing*, by passing a law that a debtor, when sued, might have whatever articles of his property he should choose appraised, and the creditor was compelled to take such articles at the valuation, or lose his debt. This law, in derision, was called the " hog-trough law," as a man might have his hog-trough appraised, and turned in to pay his debts.

One circumstance relative to the singing in the meeting-house at this period, is deserving of notice, inasmuch as it shows the carefulness of our fathers in guarding against innovations in all things pertaining to religious worship. It was the practice, previous to this time, in our churches, to have the minister select and read the psalm, or hymn, as now, then the oldest deacon would read one line, which was sung by all who could sing, sitting promiscuously in every part of the meeting-house. Then another line was read and sung in the same manner, and so on through the psalm, or hymn. It appears that in 1787, some bold innovators in psalmody undertook to introduce something similar to our present mode of singing, together with some new tunes. These latter were quite incomprehensible to some veterans whose sweet voices of fifty years' standing were hushed in consequence. They of course exclaimed against the innovation; others objected to it as irreligious and unscriptural. The point was argued with so much warmth on both sides, that it attracted the attention of the whole town. Accordingly, an article was inserted in a warrant for a town meeting, reading thus—"To see if the town will vote to come into any general rule in regard to carrying on the singing part of the public worship of God ; and whether the singers shall sing a part·of the time without reading, and how the psalm shall be read—whether by line or verse, or act anything thereon." A committee was chosen to take the thing into serious consideration, and to report at the next meeting.

The committee made the following report, which was accepted. " There shall be singing five times in the worshiping on the Lord's day, in the following manner : The first singing in the morning before prayers, shall be without reading and singing line by line. After prayers, in the singing, each line shall be read and sung separately, and such tunes shall be set as the congregation can, in general, sing. The first singing in the afternoon and before prayers, shall be without reading and singing line by line. After prayers, each line shall be read and sung separately, and after sermon, the singing shall be without reading and singing line by line." Thus happily was this difficult matter compromised. Enough of the old fashion was retained to satisfy the aged people, whose prejudices in this matter were probably imbedded in their very existence, while the taste of those who were pleased with the change was gratified by carrying three-fifths of their point.

In December of this year, (1787) Dea. Daniel Putnam was chosen to represent the town in the State Convention which was held at Boston on the second Wednesday of 1788, to deliberate on the subject matter of the new proposed Federal Constitution. He was unanimously instructed to vote in favor of the Constitution, with amendments.

Perhaps enough has already been said respecting the appearance of the centre of the town—the number and situation of the houses—to convey a tolerably accurate idea of its condition in

1786, or fifty years ago. A cursory view of it, however, may prove somewhat interesting. A traveler approaching from the east or south, would first behold the tavern of Thomas Cowdin, Esq. Upon the hill to the north-west, might be seen a small, yellow, and rather mean-looking meeting-house. In front would appear the "red store" of Joseph Fox, Esq., and in the rear of that, his dwelling house, with large projecting eaves. The mills and dwelling house of Dea. Ephraim Kimball were just below, and over the bridge were two houses more. Casting his eyes up the hill, he would see the house of Rev. Mr. Payson, where C. Marshall now lives. This was all that could be seen, and all that then constituted the middle of Fitchburg. Thence proceeding westward, over a crooked and rough road, the traveler would next see the house already mentioned as having been built by David Gibson, and opposite to that, on the right, the baker's shop. He would then come on to the present common. Here his sight would be greeted by small, stinted pine trees, and such bushes as grow upon the poorest land. A straggling log fence here and there might serve to diversify the scene. Nothing more was to be seen, unless William Brown had commenced building Capt. Z. Sheldon's present dwelling house, till passing the swell of ground at Dr. Abel Fox's house, the modest, unassuming house of Benjamin Danforth would be visible on the right, and his blacksmith's shop on the left. Continuing his course onward, over one of the most wretched roads that ever bore that name, and passing over the high bridge—and a crazy one it was—near the bellows shop of Messrs. Thurston & Battis, no marks of human habitation were to be seen, till passing round the hill, he might discern in the distance the solitary cottage of Benjamin Kemp.

The river, which is now crowded, so to speak, with mills and factories, then appeared like a useless profusion of water flowing noisily along over its rocky bed to the parent ocean, unobstructed by a single dam, save the one in the Old City. Such, fifty years ago, was the forbidding aspect of what is now the busy and pleasant village of Fitchburg.

I have been thus particular in describing the appearance of the centre of the town at this period, because then arose the contest respecting the location of a new meeting house — a contest which continued full ten years, and was conducted with more bitterness of feeling, and display of angry passions, than any other town difficulty that ever existed among us.

The wealth and business of the town is now so concentrated, that it would seem like folly to contend that the meeting house should be placed anywhere else than in, or near its present location. But from what has already been said, and from what will be hereafter explained, concerning the condition of the westerly part of the town, it will appear that those who desired the meeting house to be located further west were not so destitute of reason as one hastily judging might be inclined to suppose.

The west, at this time, was probably the most flourishing part of the town. The farmers, in selecting their locations, were guided hither by the circumstance that here was some of the best soil in the town, and that the higher grounds were not so liable to be visited by early frosts as the lower grounds on the borders of the river. The river, indeed, instead of being viewed with eyes of favor, was dreaded as a curse. Though it furnished water power for a single mill, this did not have the weight of a feather in comparison with the heavy expense of maintaining the bridges. It is not surprising, therefore, that the people of the west, burdened with no such plague within their precincts, should desire to cut themselves free from such an onerous annual tax. The tract of land now known as Dean's hill, having a good soil, and an elevation such as would strike the eye of a pioneer with delight, was early settled; and, fifty years ago, was the most flourishing part of the town.

Jacob Upton then kept quite a celebrated tavern where Capt. Dean lately lived. Jedediah Cooper also kept tavern where his son, Samuel Cooper now lives. Capt. John Upton had a store in the small house now occupied by Daniel Flint. Dr. Stone, now a distinguished physician in Harvard, and after him Dr. Ball,* practised medicine here. Near the tavern was another important appendage, a blacksmith's shop, in full operation. The land here was in a good state of cultivation, and the farmers were industrious and prosperous. The Crown Point road, which took the principal travel between Vermont and Boston, passed over this hill, and added not a little to its appearance of activity. With all these advantages and prospects, it is not surprising that the inhabitants felt their importance, and desired to exalt their condition above that of being merely an outskirt of the town of Fitchburg.

Accordingly, early in the year 1785, an article was inserted in the warrant for a town meeting—"To see if the town would take into consideration the request of Jacob Upton and others to see if the town will set off the inhabitants of the north-westerly part of Fitchburg, with their lands and privileges, free and clear from said Fitchburg, to join the extreme part of Westminster, with the north-easterly part of Ashburnham, to be incorporated into a town, to have town privileges, as other towns." If this request had been granted, the people of the new town would have erected a meeting house not far from Upton's tavern. The effect of this was well understood. The rise in the value of real estate in that vicinity, and the impulse that would be given to business by making it the middle of the town, conspired to awaken the energies of those interested in such a consummation to bring about the desired object. But it encountered many difficulties. It was too local in its nature—and notwithstanding all the energy with which it was urged in town meeting, not only the east, but every

---

*He had but little else beside his good looks to recommend him. Not being overburthened with medical knowledge or common sense, his "practice" was limited; and he curtailed his expenses in proportion. He boarded with "landlord Upton," on condition that he should pay a certain sum for every meal at which he might be present, and that he should receive a certain sum whenever he should be absent. He contrived that his visits to his patients and neighbors should be at such an hour as to secure a meal of victuals without expense to himself. Consequently, when the time of "settling" came, it appeared that the landlord was in the doctor's debt.

part of the town not included in the limits of the proposed new town, set their faces against it. They could not see the propriety of setting off that flourishing part of the town, and taking upon themselves the whole burden of maintaining the minister, bridges, &c. So they promptly voted that the article should be dismissed.

But the petitioners, acting with that zeal which is not quenched by a single repulse, but rather gathers force from opposition, made another attempt in the following May, but in a different form. This was to see if the town would " receive about a mile or more in width of land, with the inhabitants thereon, of the northerly part of the town of Westminster, bounded on the northwesterly part of Fitchburg, to be annexed thereto, to be *convened* with others of the inhabitants of said town, for the public worship of God, and to be vested with all other privileges with said town in public matters, to join with the inhabitants of said Fitchburg to build a meeting house on Ezra Upton's land," &c. (A few rods to the southeast of the house of Daniel Works.) This was an essential modification of the original plan; and instead of taking any thing from the territory of the town, would add considerable to it. Another point was conceded by proposing to place the meeting house on Ezra Upton's land, which, with the new territory, would not be far from the centre of the town. But the wise men of the east were not to be deceived by this artfully contrived plan. They well knew that if this point was conceded, it would throw so much power into the hands of the west, that they could, if they should choose, have it set off into a separate town. This article was accordingly dismissed.

These two defeats only made the people of the west more anxious to carry their point in some shape. They began to consider it an intolerable grievance to be compelled to travel over such hills and to such a distance, to attend public worship; and accordingly in March, 1786, they requested of the town, "that Rev. Mr. Payson have liberty to preach some part of the time in the year, in the westerly part of the town." This modest request was also denied—the town probably thinking that by yielding an inch, they would open a door through which they might unwillingly be thrust a mile.

In September of this year a more important movement was made. It was voted to build "a new meeting house in the centre of the town, or in the nearest convenient place" to the centre—all being aware that the old meeting house in the Old City was not in the centre. All seemed to acknowledge the necessity of building a new meeting house, although the old house had been standing but twenty years. It had never been thoroughly finished, and the winds and weather found their way into it in such a manner as to render it uncomfortable. It had rather a shabby appearance, and was too small to accommodate all the inhabitants.

It being voted to build a new meeting house, the grand difficulty now arose, to ascertain " the nearest convenient place to the centre." Strong feelings on this subject had been already excited; but before going further into this subject, it will be proper to consider what the people in the westerly part of the town, and the adjoining part of Westminster, were doing at this time. Jedediah Cooper and Jacob Upton, the two innkeepers, and of course men of great influence, together with some of their neighbors, determined to have a meeting house among themselves at any rate. Accordingly they bestirred themselves with sufficient effect to erect a frame for such a building, opposite the road which leads from Flint McIntire's to the county road, on a small plat of ground just within the limits of Fitchburg. It was subsequently covered, and public worship was occasionally held there, but it was never sufficiently finished to be worthy the name of a meeting house.*

---

*For several years previous to the building of the first parish-meeting-house, in 1796, the people of the west had preaching here, in proportion to the amount of taxes which they paid towards the support of the minister. At other times it was indiscriminately used by Methodists, Baptists,

Respecting the building and locating the new meeting house, the town, like many other public bodies, moved slow. Private interests were enlisted on both sides, and all parties seemed inclined, if they could not gratify their own wishes, to defeat those of every one else. All seemed willing that a new meeting house should be erected, but when the discussion respecting its location commenced, a magazine was sprung, and the confusion of tongues in one of our town meetings bore some faint resemblance to that of Babel.

In September, 1788, the subject of the new meeting house was again brought before the town by means of an article in the warrant—"To see if the town will erect a meeting house in the centre of the town, or receive any part of Westminster that shall be willing to join with us, and then erect a meeting house in the nearest convenient place to the centre." It appears that the people of the west were ever determined to weave into the question concerning the location of the new meeting house, the grand object of their desires, viz. the establishment of a new town; and the other inhabitants seemed equally determined that they should never accomplish their designs. At this meeting a committee was chosen to examine and find the most convenient place on which to erect the meeting house, so as to accommodate all the inhabitants. This committee consisted of Moses Hale, Dea. Daniel Putnam, Jacob Upton, Asa Perry, and Oliver Stickney. Two of these were in favor of having it in the west, two near its present location and one was neutral. At the next meeting their report was rejected. A motion was then made to place it on the site of the old one, which was also negatived. It was then voted, after much consideration, as the record says, to erect the new

Universalists, &c., &c. The proprietors suffered it to go to decay, and its shabby appearance obtained for it the appellation of the "Lord's Barn." It was sold and taken down about ten years since, and the proceeds of the sale (amounting to about $36) were divided among the proprietors, so near as they could be ascertained.

The designation of "barn" does not appear to have been very inappropriate. The naked walls and timbers, and the many swallows which made it their abiding place, rendered assembling in it sometimes quite unpleasant.

house on the nearest convenient place to the centre. It seems that this was the only point on which the town could agree. What the value of this "much consideration" was, appears by the next vote, which was to re-consider all votes hitherto passed, relating to this matter. At this point the meeting was adjourned to 9 o'clock A. M. of the next day, for the purpose probably of recruiting their bodily strength and their several forces.

On the next morning the parties came on, and again proceeded to business. The first motion was to place the new house where the old one then stood. This was negatived. A motion was then made to place the new house on the land of Ezra Upton's heirs. (Near to Daniel Works,' as already mentioned.) The house was divided in this motion "to find a true vote," as the record says. For the motion appeared 32, against it, 17. So it was determined by a vote of almost two to one, to place the house in the west. A committee was chosen to inform the people of the west of the proceedings of the town, in placing the meeting house so as to accommodate them. The same committee was invested with power to purchase the new frame erecting for a meeting house in the northwest part of the town, if that should appear best for the town's interest—otherwise they had power "to provide timber and materials for building a new meeting house in the prudentest manner for said town on said plat of ground." They were instructed to make a report of their proceedings at the next town meeting.

This was a sore discomfiture to the east, and so they considered it. They caused another town meeting to be called immediately "To see if the town will comply with a request of a number of the inhabitants of the town of Fitchburg, to grant that they, together with their respective estates and interests, may be set off from Fitchburg and annexed to Lunenburg." This shows that the people of the east were determined never to travel over the hills to the place where the new meeting house was to be erected.

Those honest people who had before voted with the west merely to preserve harmony and keep the town together, now became alarmed lest they should lose the east in their efforts to conciliate the west. They occupied an exceedingly unpleasant position. If they said the meeting house should be placed near the old one, the west threatened to make a new town. If they yielded to the west, the east showed symptoms of returning to the arms of their good parent, Lunenburg. The request of the east was promptly denied.

Meanwhile the committee above mentioned were busily employed in the duties assigned to them, notwithstanding the squally appearances in the east. They made a bargain for the frame which had been commenced in the northwest, and prepared a site on the land of Ezra Upton's heirs. Unluckily for the west, in 1788, a town meeting was called to hear the report of this industrious committee. They came forth with confidence, stating that they had purchased the aforesaid new frame, and done many excellent things—whereupon the town gravely voted not to accept their report, and, what was rather uncivil, discharged them from any further service. This was done by the peace-makers, who, becoming somewhat frightened, once more threw their influence into the eastern scale.

A committee was now chosen to find the centre of the town. They made a survey for this purpose, and reported that they found the centre, which they designated by a monument of stones, to be about thirty rods northerly from the present pound. This report was accepted; and at an adjourned meeting in December it was voted to build the meeting house in "the nearest convenientest place to the centre," as the record says. Thomas Cowdin Esqr., Phinehas Hartwell, Oliver Stickney, Daniel Putnam, and Paul Wetherbee were chosen to execute the difficult task of finding the "convenientest place," and to purchase the land of one Thomas Boynton, who then owned it. They selected a place a little below the present pound, and purchased 22½ acres of land, giving $2.33 per acre for it*—and the town approved of these proceedings.

Thus it appears that the west was now in a minority—the peace-makers having voted with the east, to prevent the latter from carrying into execution their threat of joining Lunenburg. The men of the west immediately resorted to their old scheme of having a new town or parish among themselves. They called a town meeting, "to see if the town would set off the north-westerly part of said town, as a town, beginning on Westminster line," &c. "Or, if the town should not see fit to comply with the above request, we would earnestly request of the town that they would set us off as a parish, upon honorable terms, as may be agreed upon with being annexed with adjacent parties." By reason of the rare attendance of the "requesters," this meeting was uncommonly peaceable, and the article was dismissed. July 2d, 1789, another town meeting was called, to act upon the following article—"To see if the town will set off the westerly part of said town, as a parish, upon supposition that the north part of Westminster, the east part of Ashburnham, and a small part of Ashby will consent to be annexed to this town." This was an old game and well understood. The request was answered with a prompt denial.

The east still holding the ascendancy, on the 2d day of November, 1789, the town voted to build a new meeting-house on the land purchased of Thomas Boynton, and chose a committee with full power, for this purpose. But on the 16th of the same month, the tables were turned. A vote was passed to reconsider all former votes—so that after four years of hard labor in endeavoring to erect a new meeting-house, the town found itself precisely where it began, with the exception of owning 22½ acres of real estate. This last decision was probably effected by the circumstance that the people of the west, together with those of the

---

*The present owner of this land has been offered $100 per acre for it, which he has promptly refused.

northerly part of Westminster, and a part of Ashburnham and
Ashby, had laid before the General Court a powerful petition,
for an act of incorporation into a town.

This petition set forth in glowing colors the delightful situation
of the contemplated town—how nature had lavished all her skill
upon it—how admirably adapted for a township by itself was the
noble swell of land—and that nothing in nature or in art could
exceed the grand and imposing spectacle of a meeting-house
towering from its summit, while beneath the said swell was a
region of low, sunken land, which almost cut off the petitioners
from intercourse with the rest of mankind. All this looked
exceedingly well on paper, and was presented to the General
Court in 1790. An order of court was sent to this town, and
to the others interested, to show cause, if any they had, why
the prayer of said petition should not be granted.

The town now saw the necessity of going to work in earnest.
After conferring with committees from Westminster, Ashburnham
and Ashby, the people of Fitchburg drew up a spirited remonstrance. In this remonstrance they denied every statement set
forth in the petition — alleging that the latter was entirely the
work of fancy, and a specimen of outrageous poetical license,
that the petitioners were actuated solely by interested views, that
their object was to escape from the onerous burden of contribu-
ting their just proportion towards the maintenance of some of the
most expensive bridges that were ever created. They declared
that if the petitioners should succeed in their object, the remaining portion of the town would be completely overwhelmed by that
grievous nuisance, the North branch of the Nashua.

It will be perceived that both parties understood the art of
using extravagant language ; and so equally balanced were matters
when they came before the General Court, that it was finally
decided to let them remain as they were—and so no new town
was erected on that beautiful hill.

In September, 1791, the town, having recovered breath after

this valorous contest, began to adopt measures for building a new meeting house. The old favorite motion—to erect a meeting house in the centre of the town, or "in the nearest convenientest place thereto"—was made in town meeting, and carried—yeas 41, nays 23. A committee was chosen to report to the town the plan of such a house as it might be thought advisable to build. The report of this committee recommending three years to be allowed in which to build the house, and that individuals might have an opportunity to pay for their pews with materials and labor upon it, was accepted. A committee was chosen in October to clear a place for its situation near the pound, and had full power to proceed and finish it. At another meeting in December, the town, acting with its usual consistency, dismissed this committee from any further service. So they were again as in the beginning.

In May, 1793, an attempt was made to repair the old meeting house ; but the town would not listen to such a proposition.

The inhabitants commenced operations anew in September, 1794, by voting "to erect a meeting house in the centre of said town, or in the nearest convenientest place thereto, to accommodate the inhabitants thereof for divine worship." Three disinterested individuals not belonging to the town—viz. Josiah Stearns, Esqr. and David Kilburn of Lunenburg, and Benjamin Kimball, Esqr. of Harvard, were chosen "to centre the town," as the record says, and to ascertain that hitherto undiscovered point, "the nearest convenientest place" to said centre. They found the centre of the town to be not far from the summit of the hill, nearly seventy rods to the northeast of the present town pound. But taking all things into consideration, they decided that the house should stand a little to the rear of Messrs. Thurston & Battis' present bellows shop. The town rejected this report, yeas 29, nays 36. So the opinions of interested and disinterested persons were treated precisely alike—as good for nothing.

In the following May, another attempt was made to erect a

house upon the site recommended by this committee. The vote stood yeas 45, nays 48. At this meeting a committee of twenty-one of the inhabitants was chosen to select and report to the town a suitable place, on which to build a meeting house. This committee reported in favor of the place selected by the committee of "disinterested persons." The town then voted to build a meeting house on that place, yeas 61, nays 47. A town meeting was accordingly called on the 8th of January, 1795, for the purpose of choosing a committee to purchase the ground selected. But at this meeting the town refused to choose any such committee—and so ended the project of building a meeting house there.

But the subject was not suffered to remain long at rest; for on the 26th of the same month, it was voted to erect a meeting house on the land purchased of Thomas Boynton, and to model it after the one in Leominster. It was to be completed on the last day of December, 1796. At an adjournment of this meeting, in the following July, it was voted to model the meeting house after the one (on the hill) at Ashburnham. A road, four rods wide, beginning nearly opposite to the red cotton factory, was laid out, passing up the valley in the rear of Widow Sawyer's dwelling house, to accommodate the people of the east. John Putnam Jr. entered into a contract with the town to build the meeting house.

In September, a committee was chosen to prepare the ground for the reception of the house, and to level a common before it.

In October a motion was made in town meeting to locate the meeting house "at the crotch of the roads near Capt. William Brown's." This motion was carried, yeas 44, nays 30. So it was then decided to place the house where the First Parish meeting house now stands. I have been informed that it was designed to have the house face directly "down street," and that the underpinning was laid for that purpose, but that the opposing faction mustered sufficient strength to get it faced directly to the south, and consequently cornerwise to the street.

Thus ended a contest of full ten years' duration, respecting the location of a meeting house. It was carried on with much more than the usual degree of zeal, obstinacy and bitterness of feeling which too often characterize difficulties of this nature. Passion got the control of judgment, and men seemed willing to sacrifice everything to a desire of carrying their point. So fiercely was the contest carried on, that people from the neighboring towns frequently flocked in to attend a town meeting in Fitchburg.

I have mentioned only a few of these town meetings at which this subject was the principal topic. The town records for these ten years are principally filled with accounts of them. The number of these meetings I have not taken the trouble to count, but I have been credibly informed that the town was called together *ninety-nine times* on the subject. Indeed, if any one will take the trouble to examine the records, he will find nearly an average number of ten meetings yearly. The matter was finally compromised. The people of the west were allowed to have preaching in their neighborhood in proportion to the amount of taxes which they contributed towards the support of the minister.

The meeting house, on its present location, was built during the summer of 1796. At the " raising," the inhabitants concluded—not to bury their griefs beneath the altar — but to drown them in deep potations of West India rum. For, on this occasion the town voted—and it appears to have been the only vote on t'iis subject which did not give rise to bitter contention—to purchase a barrel of West India rum, with a sufficient quantity of loaf sugar wherewith to regale and refresh all those who might be present. So gravely and systematically did they conduct this part of the ceremonies, that they chose a committee consisting of *Deacon* Daniel Putnam, *Deacon* Kendall Boutelle, *Deacon* Ephraim Kimball, Reuben Smith, Joseph Polley, Dr. Jonas Marshall, and Asa Perry, to deal out the " *grog*," with instructions if that barrel was not sufficient, to procure more at the town's expense.

The meeting house was finished, and dedicated on the 19th day of January, 1797. The dedication sermon was preached by Rev. Zabdiel Adams, of Lunenburg, there being no settled minister in this town at that time.*

In December, 1797, Dea. Daniel Putnam was chosen to represent the town in the State Convention held in Boston in the following January, to take into consideration " the subject matter of the new proposed Federal Constitution." Objections to the Constitution were reported to the town, and unanimously adopted. The representative was instructed to report these objections to the Convention, if needful. A large majority of the town afterwards voted in favor of the Constitution.

When the troubles with France broke out, in 1793, the town promptly voted to pay the soldiers that might be drafted from this place 50s. in addition to the pay they might receive from the United States.

But few incidents worthy of note, disconnected with ecclesiastical affairs, have occurred since the year 1800. Those few will be briefly alluded to.

It seems always to have been a favorite object with the people of this town to have the County of Worcester divided, so that the towns in the northern part, together with some of those in Middlesex County, might be erected into a new county. In 1798, they sent a remonstrance to the General Court against building a new Court House in Worcester, and petitioned to have the county divided. The several towns of the county voted on the question in April, 1798, by order of the General Court. In this town the vote was unanimous (77) in favor of a division. The attempt was again renewed in 1800, by conventions in Templeton and Gardner, which delegates from this town attended. The last attempt was made in 1828, when the petitions of Ivers Jewett and others were sent to the General Court. When the question was referred to the County, the votes in Fitchburg were 117 in favor of a division, and 2 against it.

*This house is now (autumn of 1836) about to be removed and a new and more elegant structure to be erected nearly on the same site.

It appears from a remonstrance sent to the General Court in 1804, that the number of legal voters at that time was 181.

In 1820, a large majority of the inhabitants were in favor of a convention for revising the Constitution of the State. To this convention Calvin Willard and John Shepley Esqrs., were appointed delegates. A majority of the voters appeared to be in favor of most of the amendments proposed by the convention.

ECCLESIASTICAL HISTORY. The history of the ecclesiastical affairs of Lunenburg, previous to the incorporation of Fitchburg, has not been kept distinct from the other affairs of the town. It will be recollected that Fitchburg was incorporated after the death of Rev. Samuel Payson, and previous to the settlement of Rev. Zabdiel Adams. While the people of Fitchburg were unable " to provide preaching among themselves," they attended meeting at Lunenburg.

In the winter of 1764-5, they had preaching for six weeks. Having no meeting-house, they were wont to assemble in the tavern of Samuel Hunt, where they listened to the teachings of Rev. Peter Whitney. Mr. Whitney, author of "The History of Worcester County," was a graduate of Harvard University, 1762, and was for a long period minister of Northboro', Mass. Rev. Peter Whitney, of Quincy, is his son, and Rev. George Whitney, of Roxbury, his grandson.

In the year 1766, there was no preaching in the town. In 1767, application was made to Rev. Messrs. Whitney, Samuel Angier and John Payson, to come and preach. Mr. Angier, (Harvard University, 1763,) gave great satisfaction, and was invited to settle. The invitation was declined partly, if not wholly, on account of some difficulty between him and Dea. Amos Kimball.

In May, 1767, the town appointed "a day of fasting and prayer in order to ask Divine assistance in giving some gentleman a call to settle in the gospel ministry in this town."

Rev. John Payson was preaching during the summer of this year, and in November he consented to become the settled minister of the place. His ordination took place January 27th, 1768. The Church was embodied on the 9th of the same month. Mr. Payson was a son of Rev. Phillips Payson, of Chelsea, and was graduated at Harvard University in 1764. He was a brother of Rev. Samuel Payson, the young and much lamented minister of Lunenburg, who died in 1763. Rev. Dr. Seth Payson, of Rindge, N. H., was his half-brother.

Mr. Payson appears to have been a man of respectable talents, of a peaceful disposition, and of devoted piety. He was fortunate in having secured, for a long period, the love and respect of his people. Fond of the peaceful walks of his profession, he knew but little of the affairs of the world, and was ill calculated to sustain its buffets. The latter years of his ministry were embittered by the inroads made among his people by the Methodists, Baptists and Universalists. These circumstances, together with a constitutional infirmity of mind, caused a great depression of spirits, which finally settled in confirmed insanity. Lucid intervals occasionally intervened. Yet he continued to preach for several years. He would go through with the public services on the sabbath with perfect propriety, when frequently there did not occur another lucid interval during the week. He discontinued preaching for a period in the spring and summer of 1792, but resumed his pastoral duties in the autumn. His infirmity increasing upon him in the summer of 1793, both the church and town united in calling a council to take into consideration their ecclesiastical affairs.* This council

---

*The bill for the entertainment of this council at the inn of Widow Hannah Cowdin is a curiosity in its way, and is as follows —

"The Venerable Council's Bill.   "Fitchburg, Nov. 11th, 1794.

28 meals of victuals at 1s. 6d....		$7.00
17 suppers " 1s.		2.83
17 breakfasts " 1s.		2.83
34 dinners " 1s. 6d....		8.50
9 suppers " 1s.		1.50
2 breakfasts " 1s.		.33
10 lodgings " 4d....		.54
Horse keeping		10.00
☞ Liquor....		7.50

" Rec'd Par't   Hannah Cowdin."

was unable to effect a reconciliation—the town refusing to accede to Mr. Payson's propositions.

In April, 1794, all parties agreed to re-assemble the former council, and to abide by its decision. The council decided that the town should pay Mr. Payson the sum of $530, and that his pastoral relations should cease. This proposition was accepted by the town on the 2d day of May, 1794 ; and Mr. Payson's connections with the town were then dissolved.

He continued to reside here without any alleviation of his unfortunate infirmity, till May, 1804, when, being on a visit at the house of his brother-in-law, in Leominster, he put a period to his existence by first taking poison, and cutting his throat immediately after. In a lucid interval before his death, he expressed the most poignant grief for the act which he had committed.* He died in the 59th year of his age, and in the 36th of his ministry.

For about one year after this period, Rev. John Kimball was employed to preach, and was invited to become the minister of the place, but the invitation was declined.

In December, 1795, an invitation given to Rev. John Miles, to "settle," was declined by him. In April, 1797, the church

---

*The following is the inscription upon the tomb-stone, in the old grave yard in this town.

"SUB HOC TUMULO
RELIQUIÆ
REV. JOHANNIS PAYSON A. M.
JACENT;
OLIM ECCLESIÆ FITCHBURGENSIS
PASTOR
QUI DIE MAII XVIII
ANNO DOMINI M. DCCCIV
MORTUUS EST,
ANNO ÆTATIS LIX
ANNOQUE SUI SACERDOTII XXXVI.
PRÆSTANTISSIMO VIR INGENIO
BENEVOLENTISSIMOQUE ANIMO
SCIENTIA PRÆDITUS, MANDATOQUE DIVINO FIDELIS,
STUDIO EXERCITATIOQUE THEOLOGIÆ
AMICO MONITU FACTISQUE CHARITATIS DUCTUS
POTIUSQUAM CONTENTIONI INANI
PERSECUTIONIBUSQUE AVARITIÆ SORDIDIS.

A SON ERECTS THIS MONUMENT TO THE MEMORY OF AN AFFEC-
TIONATE AND BELOVED FATHER."

proposed to give Rev. Mr. Noyes a "call," but the town declined, and immediately proposed, by a vote of 43 to 24, Rev. Samuel Worcester. The church concurred, and Mr. Worcester was ordained in September, 1797. He received a "settlement" of $333.33 the first year, and the same amount the second. His salary was $333.33 per annum, with the improvement of the town's land. When either party wished to give up the contract, it was stipulated that it might be done by a mutual council. A majority of the people became dissatisfied with him in 1801, and the town was divided into three societies. The time which each should occupy the meeting-house was determined by the proportion of taxes which they paid. By this rule, the society in the east part of the town occupied it 24 sabbaths, Mr. Worcester's society 17 sabbaths, the society in the west 8 sabbaths, and the Methodists and Baptists 3 sabbaths. In May, 1801, Mr. Worcester expressed a desire to be dismissed; but he and the church claimed the sole right of appointing the council—which claim the town considered to be a violation of the contract of settlement. Accordingly, in August, the town voted that they considered Mr. Worcester to be dismissed, and the contract null and void. By their order, the doors of the meeting-house were closed, and could not be opened except by order of the selectmen. In June, 1802, Mr. Worcester was dismissed by the sanction of a regularly convened council, and his pastoral relations ceased in the following September.

At this time the two parties into which the town was divided, were much imbittered against each other, and the parochial powers of the town were soon dissolved. In the Spring of 1804, Rev. Titus Theodore Barton was installed as pastor over the one society, and shortly after, Rev. Wm. Bascom became the pastor of the other.

Mr. Barton's church and society became discontented with him in 1812, in consequence of some indiscretions on his part mingled with political feelings, and he was dismissed in February, 1813. Mr. Bascom's society then made overtures for a re-union of the societies, which was effected near the close of the same year

—Mr. Bascom himself, at the same time, requesting to be dismissed. The request was granted, and in 1815 he went to Leominster.

In June, 1814, the church invited Rev. Winthrop Bailey to become their pastor, but he declined in consequence of the opposition made to his settlement by a portion of the society.

Rev. William Eaton began to preach in February, 1815, and became the settled minister of the place in August of the same year. He was dismissed June 30th, 1823, at his own request—a considerable portion of his society not agreeing with him in religious sentiments. In October, 1823, the two societies separated from each other. Rev. Calvin Lincoln, Jr., the present minister of the first society, was ordained June 30th, 1824.

Rev. Rufus A. Putnam was ordained over the "Calvinistic Congregational Church" and Society in February, 1824, and was dismissed, at his own request, in March, 1831. Rev. John A. Albro was installed pastor of the same society in May, 1832, and was dismissed, at his own request, in December, 1834. Rev. Joshua Emery, Jr., the present pastor, was ordained in May, 1835.

The meeting-house belonging to this society was built during the ministry of Rev. Mr. Barton, and was enlarged to its present size in 1828.

The Village Baptist society was formed in March, 1831, and incorporated in February, 1834. The meeting-house was built in the Autumn of 1833. Rev. Appleton Morse was hired to preach in the Spring of 1831, and continued till February, 1834. Rev. John W. McDonald was hired to preach from December, 1834, to November, 1835. Rev. O. L. Lovell, the present preacher, commenced in January, 1836.

The Methodist Society was formed in March, 1834. The first preacher was Rev. Joel Knight, who commenced his labors in this place in June, 1834, and left in the Autumn of 1835.

"The first Baptist Society of Fitchburg and Ashby"—which society has a meeting-house* in the northern part of this town—

---

*This meeting-house is not far from the limits of Ashby, on the road leading to that town. It is small in size, and not very elegant in its appearance. The traveler, not informed of the purpose for which it was erected, would probably mistake it for a barn.

was incorporated in June, 1810. Rev. Benjamin Tolman, a regularly ordained minister, has been the pastor of this society for a long period. This Society belongs to the denomination of those usually styled "Free-will Baptists," and has no connection with the Baptist society which formerly existed in the westerly part of the town. These latter were more properly "Calvinistic Baptists." So early as 1787, "seventeen professed Baptists" were exempted from paying any tax towards the support of Rev. Mr. Payson, as they had preaching among themselves. They continued to have preaching at intervals, till the strife respecting the location of the meeting-house had subsided. After that period, both the Methodists and Baptists in the west, gradually dwindled away, or united themselves with societies in other towns.

It has not been thought necessary to descend into the particulars of the unhappy difficulties which this town has experienced in its ecclesiastical affairs. The recital of them, at the present time, would prove to be rather painful than interesting, and perhaps an impartial account would give satisfaction to neither party. When it is recollected that these divisions commenced in the year 1800, during the ministry of Rev. Mr. Worcester, and continued, with more or less excitement, till the ordinations of Rev. Messrs. Putnam and Lincoln, in 1824—during which period difficulty after difficulty arose, and council after council was called; when more than one separation and union of the societies were effected, and when the church and parish frequently came into collision—it will be seen that a strictly impartial account of them would be a task of no small difficulty, and would extend the limits of this work much too far. It will be enough to state generally that angry feelings were frequently indulged to an inexcusable extent. Neighbor was divided against neighbor, family against family, and sometimes husband against wife. On one occasion, during the ministry of Mr. Worcester, a council was in session nearly a fortnight, and on another, two councils were convened at the same time. If this excited state of feeling has now passed away, the writer would not incur the hazard of disturbing the calm by galling a tender wound.

APPENDIX.

REPRESENTATIVES.

I have thought that a complete list of the Representatives of this town, since the adoption of the Constitution, might possess some interest. Previous to that period Fitchburg and Lunenburg formed one Representative district. During the period of the Revolution, the Delegates from this town to the most important Conventions are mentioned in the body of this work.

1780.........Thomas Cowdin.	1802.........Voted not to send.
1781.........None chosen.	1803.........Joseph Fox.
1782.........Voted not to send.	1804.........Joseph Fox.
1783.........Thomas Cowdin.	1805.........Samuel Gibson.
1784.........Thomas Cowdin.	1806.........Samuel Gibson.
1785.........Voted not to send.	1807.........Samuel Gibson.
1786.........Voted not to send.	1808.........Voted not to send.
1787.........Daniel Putnam.	1809.........Voted not to send.
1788.........Daniel Putnam.	1810.........Abraham Willard,
1789.........Daniel Putnam.	Paul Wetherbee.
1790.........Daniel Putnam.	1811.........Paul Wetherbee,
1791.........Daniel Putnam.	Abraham Willard.
1792.........Daniel Putnam.	1812.........Paul Wetherbee,
1793.........Daniel Putnam.	Samuel Gibson.
1794.........Voted not to send.	1813*
1795.........William Brown.	1814.........Voted not to send.
1796.........Voted not to send.	1815.........Voted not to send.
1797.........Voted not to send.	1816.........Voted not to send.
1798.........Joseph Fox.	1817.........Voted not to send.
1799.........William Brown.	1818.........Voted not to send.
1800.........Voted not to send.	1819.........Voted not to send.
1801.........Joseph Fox.	1820.........Voted not to send.

* " No one appeared to have more votes than all the rest".

1821.........Voted not to send.
1822.........Voted not to send.*
1823.........Joseph Downe, Jr.
1824.........Calvin Willard.
1825.........John Shepley.
1826.........Francis Perkins.
1827.........Francis Perkins.
     Joseph Simonds.
1828.........Francis Perkins.
     Isaiah Putnam.
1829.........Isaiah Putnam.
     Oliver Fox.
1830.........Isaiah Putnam,
     Payson Williams.
1831.........Zachariah Sheldon,

     Isaiah Putnam,
     Zachariah Sheldon,†
     Ebenezer Torrey.†
1832.........David Boutelle,†
     Abiel J. Towne,†
     Levi Farwell.†
1833.........David Boutelle,†
     Francis Perkins,†
     Isaiah Putnam.†
1834.........Isaiah Putnam,†
     Levi Farwell,†
     Enoch Caldwell..†
1835.........Isaiah Putnam,†
     Alvah Crocker,†
     Enoch Caldwell.†

VOTES FOR GOVERNOR,

Given in Fitchburg, since the adoption of the Constitution. "Scattering" votes are omitted.

1780—John Hancock,..............63   James Bowdoin,......................1
1781—John Hancock,..............35
1782—John Hancock,..............16   James Bowdoin,.....................3
1783—John Hancock,..... 37   James Bowdoin,......................1
1784— { Rev. Zabdiel Adams,.....21   { John Hancock,....................2
      { Samuel Holton, ...17   { John Adams,......................1
1785—Samuel Holton, ...16   Thomas Cushing, ...:............6
1786—Samuel Holton, ...12   Thomas Cushing, ...4
1787—John Hancock,..............56   James Bowdoin,.....................5
1788—John Hancock,..............39   Elbridge Gerry, ...12
1789—John Hancock,...........~59
1790—John Hancock,..............48
1791—John Hancock,..............39   Francis Dana,.....................1
1792—John Hancock,..............50   Azor Orne,........................4
1793—John Hancock,..............39
1794—Samuel Adams, ...60   Elbridge Gerry, ...2
1795—Samuel Adams, ...52
1796—Samuel Adams, ...67
1797—James Sullivan, ...27   Moses Gill,......................9

*The Town was fined this year for not sending.   †Chosen in November.

1798—James Sullivan,	43	Increase Sumner,	4
1799—William Heath,	57	Increase Sumner,	16
1800—Elbridge Gerry,	64	Caleb Strong,	12
1801—Elbridge Gerry,	60	Caleb Strong,	37
1802—Elbridge Gerry,	72	Caleb Strong,	70
1803—Elbridge Gerry,	63	Caleb Strong,	63
1804—James Sullivan,	74	Caleb Strong,	59
1805—James Sullivan,	87	Caleb Strong,	82
1806—James Sullivan,	112	Caleb Strong,	76
1807—James Sullivan,	113	Caleb Strong,	95
1808—James Sullivan,	105	Christopher Gore,	94
1809—Levi Lincoln,	132	Christopher Gore,	113
1810—Elbridge Gerry,	130	Christopher Gore,	103
1811—Elbridge Gerry,	129	Christopher Gore,	90
1812—Elbridge Gerry,	141	Caleb Strong,	126
1813—Joseph B. Varnum,	141	Caleb Strong,	136
1814—Samuel Dexter,	149	Caleb Strong,	145
1815—Caleb Strong,	142	Samuel Dexter,	136
1816—Samuel Dexter,	148	John Brooks,	134
1817—Henry Dearborn,	124	John Brooks,	123
1818—John Brooks,	116	B. W. Crowninshield,	97
1819—John Brooks,	122	B. W. Crowninshield,	111
1820—John Brooks,	107	William Eustis,	103
1821—William Eustis,	99	John Brooks,	97
1822—William Eustis,	106	John Brooks,	97
1823—William Eustis,	111	Harrison G. Otis,	107
1824—William Eustis,	142	Samuel Lathrop,	123
1825—Levi Lincoln,	111		
1826—Levi Lincoln,	64	Samuel Hubbard,	58
1827—Levi Lincoln,	118	Marcus Morton,	15
1828—Levi Lincoln,	73	Marcus Morton,	3
1829—Marcus Morton,	59	Levi Lincoln,	40
1830—Levi Lincoln,	97	Marcus Morton,	72
1831—Levi Lincoln,	64	Marcus Morton,	64
1831—(Nov.) L. Lincoln,	93	Samuel Lathrop,	75
1832—Levi Lincoln,	124	{ Samuel Lathrop,	49
		{ Marcus Morton,	27
1833—Marcus Morton,	133	{ John Davis,	127
		{ John Quincy Adams,	37
1834—John Davis,	195	Marcus Morton,	82
1835—Edward Everett,	151	Marcus Morton,	85

FULLNAME INDEX

www.ingramcontent.com/pod-product-compliance
Lightning Source LLC
Chambersburg PA
CBHW060400090426
42734CB00011B/2197